DIY RV Solar Power

How To Install Your Own Solar Power System For Your RV, Camper, or Boat

Mike Holsworth

Table Of Contents

Introduction

This book is about using solar in your RV, boat, van, or something along those lines. Mobility, remoteness, and high power requirements are the three elements they have in common. It turns out these elements make a significant difference when it comes to the things you have to consider, how you go about installation, the equipment that is needed, and the way you use and maintain it.

Most people think of solar and instantly visualize the panels that go on top. Well, yes, that's part of the story. There are so many other things that go into making sure that when you go to turn on a switch in your RV in the dead of night in winter or in the middle of nowhere, your heater comes on. From the collectors up top to the wires and junction boxes, batteries, and other equipment, there is a lot for you to put together, and that's what we are here to walk you through.

The bulk of the system includes the panels and the batteries. The panels collect the sunlight, but you need to be able to store the electricity that it makes, and the batteries are an important part of the discussion. We look at that first, after discussing some of the terminologies that you will need to equip yourself with. Once you get a handle on the batteries, then we move on to looking at the solar panels and how to balance the panels you need with the load-bearing ability of your vehicle. We will also look at selecting the necessary inverter, the proper wire gauge, and the required power meters. We will also look at backup powers and how to integrate them in the circuit. There are a couple of ways you can choose to do this. If you want to charge the batteries with the generator, you will have to hook it up in one way, but if you just want to send the power from the generator to your rig directly, then there is another way you can do it.

Once you are all hooked up, there are still issues that you need to consider, especially where and how you should direct the panels and what would be the best way to optimize your charge rates.

Finally, we look at how to keep your system maintained and the best practice involved in using them. We try to set up the whole rig with a maintenance-free philosophy, but even the most hands-off system is going to need some form of upkeep and care.

With that, let's get started and dive straight into it.

Chapter 1: What is Solar Power?

Most of us already understand the meaning of solar power—the extraction of energy from the light of the sun. We also understand that having solar power on the roofs of our homes can provide us with the power to offset our use, and in many cases, we are even able to sell power back to the utility company. For that reason, whatever amount of electricity you generate at home you use, then you charge your batteries, and if you are still able to generate more, you are free to sell back to the power company. This is the key difference when it comes to solar power for RVs. At some point, the bank of batteries that you have in your vehicle reaches its maximum. Once you reach the maximum storage, you have no longer any need for stored energy, because in an RV, you can't sell the power back to the utility company.

The next difference which we touched in passing just now is that there are only so many batteries that you can carry on your RV. In your home, you can have as many batteries as you wish. The limitations on batteries are not just about costs, it's also about weight and space.

Finally, it's about how you use your RV. In home solar, how you use power is important. But it is only one dimension of the issue. At home, you only need to consider what you use after the sun sets and then think about your capacity from there. But on an RV, there are more factors to consider.

At its crux, boats, RVs, and trailers have one thing in common—they are not planted to the ground like a house is. This reason alone requires that you solve all the issues that arise with solar power and installations differently across all platforms and think about them uniquely.

I have two other powerful books on solar, one titled *Solar Power: Making the Smart Switch to Solar Power—And Staying Within Budget!* with the other being *Solar Power: How To Harness The Sun To Power Your Life – And Go Off-Grid While Doing It.* You can refer to those if you want to get some basic ideas on electricity and solar that remain the same across platforms, but if you are specifically looking to install it in any mobile vehicle, then you need to rethink it from scratch.

This book looks at solar exclusively from a mobile perspective. It sets up how you need to think about solar and the considerations you have to make when you are on the move. Unlike home systems that can grab power from the grid, depending on where you in your vehicle, a grid may not be at hand—like, say, when you are out on the water.

Your electricity profile is influenced by three factors: how you use it, how much you use, and the conditions in which you use it. That goes for home use, and it goes for mobile use. If you are setting up solar or a manufacturing plant, then the considerations are very different from the one that would need to be taken to design a home system. In the same way, how you use your RV, or your boat for that matter, is something that you need to take seriously.

Solar energy essentially means photovoltaic power. *Photo*, referring to the sun, and *voltaic*, referring to the power potential that it creates. In 1887, Heinrich Hertz discovered that if you shine ultraviolet light on electrodes, bringing two of them together causes greater arcing. The idea of light and electricity was born, and even Einstein postulated the photoelectric effect. There are some similarities to photoelectric and photovoltaic circuits. They are both very similar in the fact that light hits them, and they generate electricity. The difference is that photovoltaic circuits are a closed loop. The ejected electron moves in the circuit to do its work and then returns to the starting point cell. In a photoelectric circuit, the electron, or charge carrier, does not return.

All energy that we harvest in the world, whether it is from crude oil, hydroelectric, wind, or even when you burn coal or wood, can be traced back to the energy from the sun. It is calculated that the earth receives almost 180,000 terawatts of energy. On a clear day at noon, with the sun directly overhead, the surface receives approximately 1,000 mW per square meter. There are a number of factors that affect this peak number. As you may expect, clouds, rain, even dust, as well as the location on the earth and the time of day have an impact. When the sun goes beyond the horizon, that output effectively goes to zero. In between those two extremes, the sunlight hits that point at increasing angles and at increasing thickness of gravity, reducing the intensity of photons hitting the spot—just like how the sun at noon results in more light and heat than at dusk or dawn.

With a house always subjected to the same range of relative sun and the average days of clear skies, it is easy to get an estimate of how much contribution solar panels will make to your energy consumption profile. When you are traveling, however, there are two things that complicate that estimate. The first is the location that you are traveling to (which has bearing on all the things we mentioned about house location), and the second is how often you park and if you generate electricity while you drive.

The Terminology in Layman's Terms

My books that I mentioned in the last section have a good section on the terminology that you would have to brush up on in order to be able to communicate about and read up on all the necessary components that will go into the setting up of your RV's solar power generators.

Here, I will review some of them just so that you get a basic idea of how all this comes together.

Albedo - the ratio of light that is absorbed versus light that is reflected.

Alternating current (AC) - current that constantly reverses direction at specific intervals.

Altitude - height above the ground.

Ampere (amp) - a unit of current (number of charge-carrying particles) that flows past a certain point in a period of time (one second).

Array - modules of PV cells strung together to increase the amount of electricity in the circuit.

Azimuth - horizontal angle measured clockwise in degrees from a reference direction, usually the north or south point of the horizon to the point on the horizon intersected by the object's line of altitude.

Cell - smallest unit found in photovoltaic panels. Multiple cells form a panel.

Diffuse insolation - describes solar radiation that is scattered from striking atmospheric components.

Direct current (DC) - electrons flow only in one way as opposed to alternating (AC) current.

Direct insolation - describes solar radiation that directly hits the earth's surface.

Electrical efficiency - the ratio of power output to total power consumed.

Electric circuit - electrons start and end up in the same place after doing the work it is required to do (i.e., light a bulb, run a motor, etc.). That path is a closed circuit.

Electric current - measured in amps, or amperes, it is the rate of electric charge flow.

Electrical grid - the network of users, transmission lines, power plants, and other relevant interconnected equipment set up for the purpose of power distribution.

Gigawatt (GW) - 1,000,000,000 watts.

Insolation - refers to the amount of solar radiation received at a given area on earth.

Inverter - a device that converts direct current to alternating current.

Junction box - a protected enclosure for electrical wire connections that can be easily accessed.

Kilowatt (kW) – 1,000 watts.

Kilowatt-hour (kWh) - the measure of 1,000 watts of power production in hours.

Load - either the power consumed by a device or the resistance introduced to a circuit.

Megawatt (MW) - one million watts.

Module - also known as a panel, it is a collection of solar cells.

Monocrystalline - a single crystal of silicon; they are highly effective and are known to be the most efficient among the available technology today.

Ohm - unit that describes a measure of electrical resistance.

Photovoltaic (PV) - cell and panels that convert solar radiation into electricity.

Photovoltaic efficiency - calculated by taking the power of the sun that hits the panels and then referencing that with the power that is generated from the solar cells. PV efficiency is affected by many things including the material that is used to make the cells, the temperature of the panels, and the surrounding area as well as the age and design of the system.

Photovoltaic system - or PV system that uses solar panels made of solar cells to convert the sun's light into electricity.

Polycrystalline cell - when a solar cell is made from liquid silicon then solidified to form multiple crystals of silicon.

Radiance - the visible light that we see coming from the sun.

Remote system - as used in this book, it is a PV system that is not connected to a power grid. When traveling, all mobile systems are considered remote.

Silicon - an element found in the periodic table with the symbol Si.

Solar or sol - anything pertaining to the sun.

Solar constant - a theoretically derived number that takes an average measurement of solar radiation density as measured just beyond earth's atmosphere. It is approximated at 0.14 watts per square centimeter.

Solar energy - solar radiation that is used to derive power.

Solar power - sun's energy that is extracted into electrical energy.

Solar spectrum - spectrum of wavelengths that make up the visible and invisible light of the sun.

Solar thermal - refers to the methods used to capture solar energy coming from heat energy.

Thin film - a layer of semiconductor material that is paper thin. Typically, this is made of amorphous silicon that is layered directly onto plate glass. Not an efficient setup.

Tracking array - an array of solar panels that automatically track the movement of the sun to maximize the angle in which the sunlight hits the surface.

Transformer - a device used to move electricity from one circuit to another; DC and AC systems require a different kind of transformer.

Volt (V) – the standard unit of voltage (see below). One volt is the flow of one ampere of current when there is a resistance of one ohm.

Voltage - the potential energy that exists within a circuit, like a waterfall where the water moves from higher ground to lower ground. That potential is responsible for the electrical current found in a circuit when it is pushed around the circuit.

Watt (W) - the measure of a unit of electrical power. It is also considered to be the amount of work (Joules) per unit of time. For instance, one amp of current at one volt results in one watt of power.

Benefits of Solar Power

There are a number of benefits to using solar power. Some of these are widely known and accepted, but they are listed here anyway in the hopes that those who are not aware of solar power or their benefits learn about them.

1. It is cost-effective. Once the initial installation and equipment costs are incurred, there are minimal service and maintenance costs that follow.

2. The power generated is clean. There are no pollutants associated with the power or the generation process.

3. The power is quiet. There are no moving parts or systems that generate any amount of sound.

4. The equipment has no moving parts and thus no wear and tear to speak of, which leads to minimal replacement costs over long periods of time—up to 20 to 30 years.

5. The use of solar panels extends the life of your RV or boat batteries.

6. Installation is easy to carry out.

As you will see as we make our way through the rest of the book, you should be able to install your own solar system on your RV, boat, or van. There are some things that may confuse you along the way, but the community in the solar space is so accommodating that the same salesman that you make your purchase from is going to most likely help you integrate his product with your setup, so you will come away from all this with a good system. One of the things I highly encourage is to run your solar system that you set up in your backyard every day for a week. It's actually quite fun to go out back and run your devices; it's kind of like camping in your backyard.

Chapter 2: What is Electricity, and How is it Measured?

In simple terms, electricity is the movement of electrons or charged particles in a circuit. There is electricity all around us and even within us. We use electricity to accomplish work, because electricity is one of the easiest forms of energy that can be transported long distances. We have muscular energy in humans, but that's not so easily transported.

To understand electricity, we need to start with something a little more basic— elements. All elements are made up of atoms. You find elements on the periodic table. Atoms consist of protons, neutrons, and electrons. We are all familiar with the atom from high school. It consists of a proton and neutrons that form the core, and electrons that orbit around it. All of that—the protons and the neutrons in the center, and the electrons as well as the space between them—are all part of what we come to know as the atom. An atom is not stationary. It's not like having a grain of sand. That grain of sand (not considering that it is also made of atoms) is a stationary object. If you could see an atom, you would see that it is dynamic—constantly moving and constantly changing. The only time that it comes to a stand-still is when you freeze it to absolute zero.

The least number of protons found in an atom is one. An atom that has one electron in orbit and one proton in the nucleus is the hydrogen atom. It is the lightest element in nature. Protons have mass and charge. Electrons have mass and charge as well. Neutrons have mass but negligible charge. Each particle has its own particular charge—protons are positive, electrons are negative, and neutrons are neutral.

The protons in the nucleus attract the electrons that are in orbit. The electrons occupy different shells, which is another way of referring to the altitude of the electron from the proton. For this part, you can imagine the planets that orbit the sun. Each shell on the atom is like the different orbit of planets, except in electrons each shell can house more than one electron. The outermost shell holds electrons that are called the valence electrons. These outermost electrons experience the least amount of attraction from the nucleus of the atom and are the easiest to pull away.

Volts

When that electron is pulled away and travels along a path, it has to move in a certain direction. That direction is determined by an electric field. The details of this are beyond the scope of this book, but the point that you must take with you is that the electron will move from the area of high concentration to an area of low concentration. The greater the difference between the higher and the lower, the greater the potential. The greater the potential between the two ends, the stronger the push of electrons in the circuit from the high to the low. That potential is described by volts. You hear it often that something is 12V, 24V, or 110V. This is often described by analogies using water pressure to illustrate volts. Take a tank that has two chambers separated by a valve. On one side there is no water, and on the other side, there is about three feet of water in the chamber. The pressure exerted by the three-foot column will make the water push into the empty chamber. It will start off with more pressure and as the column gets lower, it pushes less until the two chambers have the same height of water. At that point, there is no more push. There is no longer any difference in the pressure of the two.

In almost the same way (but not exactly), when a circuit is closed, the electron is pushed from the start to move and that knocks out the electron in the atom closest to it. That electron then goes to the neighboring atom and knocks out the electron in its outermost shell. That keeps happening along the length of the entire circuit. The easier it is to knock an electron off its atom, the more conductive the material is. The more difficult it is to knock an electron off its outer shell, the less conductive it is.

So think about that for a second. When you get a solar generator, what are you actually doing with the electricity? You are not capturing electricity from the sun. Instead, you are using the photons to knock off electrons in the solar cell, and that electron then makes its way around the circuit. It's not the heat of the sun that is making electricity. You could generate electricity in the dead of winter as long as you have sufficient sunlight.

When you have a battery, the voltage of that battery tells you how much push it has. Imagine a trolley is carrying a couple of robots. That trolley moves through hurdles and traffic to get to different areas of the city to deliver the robots to do mechanical work. The trolley is pushed past obstacles and friction, then gets to its destination. The robots get down and go do the work then get back in the trolley and go home. If you have a huge bodybuilder, say Arnold Schwarzenegger in his prime, you will be able to push that car easily. If, instead, you get someone like Pee Wee Herman to do it, he wouldn't be able to push much of a load. If you get a toddler, then the possibility that the kid can move the trolley even a little is an issue. The force is what voltage is. It tells you how much of a load it can push through. Arnold would have much greater voltage than the toddler.

Current

The second thing in electricity that you hear all the time is amps. Amps is short for ampere. This is the measurement of current. So the next question is then, what is current? Simply put, current is the rate of charge flow.

If you recall, electricity is the movement of charge. Charges are either positive or negative. Protons are positively charged, and electrons are negatively charged. When we speak of electricity, we speak of the movement of electrons carrying that negative charge. Amps measure how many of those charged particles are moving through the circuit or, more specifically, across the point that is being measured. That could change in different parts of the circuit.

If you take a cross-section of a cable, you will find that it has a certain area. That area gives you an idea of how many charged particles can pass through the conduit. If you recall, electricity is about the movement of charged particles, and they move by knocking electrons off the outer shell of an electron. In a copper wire, the electron at the back is knocked out by an electron behind it. It knocks out the electron and that electron comes to the next atom in front of it. As such, if you could know how many atoms there were in a particular cross-section, you could then know how many electrons are getting bumped at any point in time.

Imagine a room full of kids. That room is connected to another equal-sized room that is empty by a tunnel that can fit exactly four kids side by side. If the kids walked at a normal pace, they would get into the tunnel, walk the distance, then enter the second room. They would enter it at a rate of four kids at a time. If each row of kids entered each second, then you will have the room filled up at a rate of four kids per second. If you released a scary monster to "push" the kids to move faster through the tunnel, then they would start running, and then three rows would enter the room each second. In other words, 12 kids would enter the room per second. In the first case, it was 4 kids per second, and in the second case, it was 12. The greater the push at the back, the greater the rate of kid movement. The kids are like the charged particles, and the monster in the first room is what's making them move faster—the greater voltage. But there is a limit to that. You can't keep increasing the size of the monster and expect the kids to run faster. It will come a time when the increase in monster size would not be met with increased running speed by the kids.

The only way you could now make an increased rate of flow would be to increase the size of the tunnel. That would be similar to increasing the diameter of the wire. To a certain extent, that would make a difference. It will allow more charged particles to flow at a given time and allow the appliance to pull as much electricity as it needed. The more work that needs to be done by the appliance or the motor, or whatever else that needs the electricity to work, the more charged particles it is going to need.

When you increase the diameter of the wire, the cross section of the wire now has more atoms, and that means it can act as a wider bridge for the electrons to travel. The more dense the wire or the larger the diameter, the more atoms it will contain, which will allow more charged particles to move along the path.

One more thing you will have to consider is that if the wire is long, meaning that the distance between the power source and the power use is farther apart, then the wire that transmits the power between them acts also as a resistor.

For every meter of wire, there is a resistance that is added to the circuit. The longer the wire, the more the resistance, and because of that more voltage is needed to push the charge through. You also need to remember that if you have a high level of resistance, you not only need more force but also more charge. So as the length of the cable increases, you need to increase the voltage at the source to push it, and you need an increased amperage to have more charge to be pushed through.

Volts, amperes, and ohms are the measurement units of voltage, current, and resistance respectively. They have a specific and unalterable relationship. Voltage is the product of current and resistance. In other words, V = I x R. Where V is voltage in volts, I is current in amps, and R is resistance in ohms. In this relationship, if you have high resistance, then you need to increase the voltage to be able to keep the current constant. If you want to keep the voltage constant, then you will have to reduce the current.

In the same way, I = V / R. It is the same thing, just rearranged with respect to I. In this case, to keep I constant, any changes in voltage must have an inverse change in resistance. So to keep amps constant, a higher resistance requires a higher voltage.

Resistance

In the same way R = I / V. In this case, to keep resistance constant, any increase in current must be accompanied by an increase in voltage. You just need to keep this relationship in mind. But there is one aspect of all this that can confuse many people. Voltage is typically fixed. You either live in a country that gets 110V or 220V out of the wall. You can’t really change the voltage, so that is typically fixed. What you can change are amps and ohms. Amps are more about what is pulled rather than what is pushed. It's better to think of amps being pulled, volts doing the pushing, and resistance being stationary. Using these three states gives you an idea of how to control them. If you need more voltage, then change the number of batteries in a battery-driven system. In terms of amps, if you get a motor to go faster, it is going to pull the amps it needs to run the motor. That increased amp requires lower resistance when the voltage remains the same. But since the wall outlet still has the same voltage, when you go to increase the amps what you realize is that the wires start to heat up. That is why fuses melt. The increased heat melts the filament and the circuit breaks. To reduce the resistance, you will have to increase the size of the cable, and that would reduce the resistance.

The greater the diameter of the cable, the less the resistance and the more current will be able to pass through it without it increasing in temperature.

When it comes to homes and mobile platforms like boats, RVs and such, always make sure that you get a licensed wireman or electrical expert to calculate the length of the wire in the circuit so that you can end up with the optimal wire gauge. Using wire that is too thin can be a fire hazard, and that is more expensive than the initial outlay of better quality cable. There are a couple of other basic issues that we should cover, and you can find them in my earlier book, as mentioned above.

Power

Power usually means something else when we use it in everyday conversations. In electricity, power has a specific meaning. Power is about the force that voltage and current create. Remember, current is the number of charged particles that flow per unit time, and volt is the force that pushes the electrons. Power is the force and the quantity that results from certain volts and certain amps. 12 amps at 110 volts result in 1,320 watts. Power is voltage times current or volts times amps. A 110-watt light bulb on the 110-volt system means that it is drawing 1 amp. A 5-amp appliance on a 12-volt source will give you 60 watts. It's not that difficult to calculate wattage. Volts—amps—watts.

Amp-Hours

We know that amps measure the quantity of charged particles transmitted in a particular circuit. If you think of a battery as a bag holding packets of energy, you should think of them as holding charged particles. If you used one amp for an hour, then that's one amp-hour. If you consume half an amp for two hours, that's also one amp-hour. Another way of looking at this is that 1 amp is one coulomb per second. 1 coulomb is 6.25×10^{18} electrons. As such, 1 Amp is 6.25×10^{18} electrons per second. This means that in one hour, a 1-amp system sends out $6.25 \times 10^{18} \times 3{,}600$ electrons per hour. That means that there are 2.25×10^{22} electrons moving in one amp-hour. I put it to you this way to make the conversation real. It feels like we are inundated with all these terms and concepts that have no way of being visualized. But with this, you can think of packets of energy—just to help you visualize. Amp-hours is a good way to look at how much all your appliances are going to use up in a night and see if you can replace it all back again during the following day.

Chapter 3: Mobile Power Setups for Your Vehicle

Setting up your mobile power system can be fun and exciting if you know what you are doing, are willing to adhere to safety guidelines, and are willing to make some mistakes along the way. Or, if you can, get a licensed installer to do the work and just shadow him while he does his thing. Your first task is to understand the specs and the use of the mobile system you are setting up. If you are setting up for a home, like we talked about in my last book, then your considerations will be very different than if you are setting up for a boat, an RV, or a van. The second layer of questions should address the size of the vehicle.

The framework that you need to underscore the thought process is to remember that you can only get out what you put in. What you put in is limited by the amount of sunlight you get and for the time you get it. It's like filling a pail you can only fill when it rains or drizzles. If it drizzles, the bucket fills up slowly. If it pours, the bucket fills up quicker. After the bucket is full, if it keeps raining—either pouring or drizzling—it makes no difference to the bucket. That bucket will overflow and only the capacity of that bucket will be all that you have. In the same way, once your batteries are filled, all the sun in the world is not going to be able to get you more.

So what does this tell us? The first thing it tells us is that there is an optimal level of solar panels that you can use. It is also limited by how much real estate you have to put it on. If your roof is only 30 square feet, then that's all you are going to be able to install.

Once you have installed that, you have to remember that the sun will be "drizzle" in the early part of the day, rise to its peak when the sun is at the zenith, then start to taper off to a trickle by the time dusk arrives. So you have a bell curve for the amount of solar energy you can collect.

You then have to think about the weather. If it is cloudy or raining heavily, then the panels are not going to be able to pick up much sunlight. At that point, the batteries, which act like a reservoir, will deplete faster than they recharge, resulting in a net outflow. But this is still better than not having any incoming power.

There are a few things that change this equation. The first is efficiency. If your solar panels are highly efficient, then that will compensate for square footage and cloudy days. The second is the type of battery. If you have high-quality batteries, then they will be able to recharge more and at a faster rate. Finally, it depends on what you are using it for and if you have some kind of usage monitor that shuts off unnecessary stuff when there is lower charge or when there are low battery levels. This is one of the most important things that you can have—active power management to extend the use of your batteries.

Up to this point, we have looked at the whole exercise in theoretical terms and conceptual frameworks. Now, we get started with the reality of it and the practical aspects of getting it designed and installed. The first is a short questionnaire that you should review so that you can get an idea of what to do.

1. Will you be installing or do you already have a generator as a backup?
2. Will you be using your vehicle in predominantly cold places, or will you be parking and visiting places that have severe or depressed temperatures?
3. What is the head count of those who will be on board?
4. What kinds of appliances run in your vehicle?
5. Do you use campgrounds or marinas to plug in and charge your batteries?
6. What is the total amp usage for all the appliances that will be used in your vehicle?

Always save the booklet that comes with all your appliances when you purchase them. This is a good place to troubleshoot, but for now, it will tell you how many amps each of your appliances are. Here is how you can work it out, shown in an example. You can print this out and use your own appliances to get an idea.

Worksheet - Power Consumption				
Item	Typical Current (amps)	X	Hours per day	Amp-Hour Consumption
4 bulb (50 watts)	16	X	12	192
CB receiver	0.5	X	2	1
Stereo	1	X	8	8
Satellite receiver	2	X	5	10
Cooling/Heating	1.2	X	12	14.4
Forced Air Furnace	8	X	10	80
Vent & Range Fan	2	X	2	4
Water Pump	8	X	2	16
DC Fridge	6	X	24	144
Microwave Oven	125	X	1	125
Blender	15	X	1	15
Hair drier 1200w	100	X	0.5	50
Total				659.4

So if all you are going to use is 656.9 amp-hours in a day, then that's the minimum storage you are going to need. Each camper or sailor is going to have different requirements and different safety margins. It also makes a difference if this is your only mechanism or if you have a fuel-driven generator to supplement your electrical needs. Many campers have a couple of strategies. They do the bulk of their charging on bright sunny days, and whatever more they need, they supplement it with generators. But I personally am not a fan of generators as they are loud, and they have both petroleum odor as well as exhaust fumes emanating from them. I'd rather use batteries charged by solar or charged at the marina or campground.

Worksheet - Power Consumption				
Item	Typical Current (amps)		Hours per day	Amp-Hour Consumption
		X		
		X		
		X		
		X		
		X		
		X		
		X		
		X		
		X		
		X		
		X		
		X		
Total				

With the above table, make a list of all the things that you have in your boat, van, or RV and then refer to the manufacturer's booklet to get the amp information. Once you have that, get an estimate of how long you use each item on a given day. You really should have two lists. The first list should be for use during daylight hours, and the second list should be for night hours. Once you have an idea of your consumption profile, you will get an idea of the capacity of batteries that you will need to install.

With that done, it brings us to battery packs or power banks. All the charging in the world needs to be stored somewhere, and that's where the batteries come in.

Item	Watts	Amps
AM/FM Cassette	8	0.1
Air Conditioner - Roof Top 13500 BTU	1600	14
Blender	300	2.6
Blow Dryer (Hair)	1500	13
Can Opener	300	2.6
CD/DVD Player	100	0.9
Clock Radio	50	0.4

Coffee Maker (10 cups)	1200	10.4
Corn Popper	600	5.2
Laptop	75	0.7
Printer	240	2.1
Crockpot	250	2.2
Curling Iron	800	7
Electric Blanket	500	4.3
Electric Fry Pan	1200	10.4
Electric Water Heater (6 gallons)	1440	12.5
Fan	300	2.6
Furnace Fan (1/3 HP)	1200	10.4
Heating Pad	250	2.2
Hot Plate	1200	10.4
Iron	1500	13
Microwave	2000	17.4
Power Converter	800	7
Refrigerator/Freezer	1200	10.4

Satellite Dish & Receiver	250	2.2
Shaver	35	0.3
Space Heater	1500	13
Stereo	100	0.9
Toaster	1500	13
Toaster Oven	1200	10.4
TVs-25" Color	300	2.6
Vacuum	1100	9.6
VCR	60	0.5
Waffle Iron	1200	10.4
Washer/Dryer	1900	16

The list above should give you an idea of the wattage that you can figure out using your calculations. This would be the same when applied to boats, RVs, and vans. The one thing that you might want to convert at this point is the watts to amp-hours. If you recall, watts is the product of volts and amps. So if you know your wattage, divide wattage by your voltage. In this case, it is 12 volts and that will give you your amps. Something that uses 1,200 watts on a 12V system means you are using 100 amps. If you use it for 2 hours per day, then that works out to be 400 amp-hours.

This gets you to understand what your consumption profile looks like in both watts and amp-hours. Once you have that, then picking a battery gets easier.

Battery Packs (rechargeable)

There are a variety of batteries on the market—everything from the one that your kid uses in his RC car to the battery in your shaver, the battery in your car, and the various batteries that go in the boat, RV, van, and so on. All batteries do one thing—they supply current to something that you wish to power. That is their single purpose. But, as you already know, that is where the simplicity ends. Beyond that, batteries can get extremely diverse and sophisticated, with everything from simple NiCad batteries to complex Li-ions used in advanced aircraft. Along the same vein of diversity, you will find many different quality products, different mission-specific products, various capacities, and even batteries that range from totally hands-off, to ones that require constant care and maintenance. For most people, the final choice is a balance of a number of factors, like cost and features.

In this book, we have two main concerns, or what we can call "critical mission parameters." There are others, but we will introduce them as we get underway. The first is that it is for mobile and remote systems. Mobile systems indicate that the rig is not stationary and will most likely be on the move. Remote means that it is going to be off the grid frequently. The reason these are not the same thing is that it is possible to be stationary and remote—like if you live on a ranch off the grid. That case wouldn't be mobile, but it would certainly be remote.

RVs, vans, and boats will typically have solar systems that are remote and mobile.

Right off the bat, we have to distinguish the batteries that go under the hood and the battery that goes in the power bank. They are two different batteries due to different missions. The one under your hood uses only a fraction of its total capacity, but when it is called upon, it has to be ready with a burst of power to turn the engine over.

The one that powers the RV appliances and equipment are the exact opposite. There is not much burst of energy required like the starter, and the power is discharged over a longer period of time until it runs out. This is called deep-cycling. The first takes huge amounts of power in bursts, and the later takes small amounts of power over long periods of time. The latter lasts longer than the one under the hood.

We will not be talking about the starter batteries that go under the hood. We will focus on the deep-cycling batteries that you will hook up to the solar panels. The next thing you need to think about is the number of amps you are going to be putting on it between charges. That's where the worksheet comes in handy. Get your list together, and use amp-hours or convert from Watts to get the total amp-hours you need based on your usage patterns between charges. In my sample up top, I need 660 amp-hours—raw. Raw, in this case, means that there is no room for wastage or error. You definitely need to have a buffer on top of that, and it depends on your budget as well. I put a 50% buffer on top of mine, because I do travel in the winter and go north to some pretty cold places. There is still good sunlight, but it occurs for fewer hours in the day, with a higher inclination. It is also really cold, so the batteries are a little less efficient.

So remember to adjust for all these items, and catch it in the buffer.

That means you now need to think about a system that can give you 660 amp-hours plus 50% of 660. So, in total, you need batteries that can give you 990 amp-hours for all the things that are on my list above. Your list, and thus your amp-hours, may be totally different—remember this is just for illustration.

You're not going to get a single battery that is going to give you 1000 amp-hours. Here comes your next issue. Most people don't realize that batteries behave differently when hooked up in series as compared to when they are hooked up in parallel.

The thing that you have to know when you set up batteries in series is that you increase the voltage only, but their amps, and thus their amp-hours, remain the same as just having one. So if you took ten 12v 100Ah batteries and put them in series, you will get 120V and 100Ah. That's not what you are looking for. What you want with a string of batteries is to keep the voltage the same but increase the amps and the amp-hours. For that, you need to place them in parallel.

When you place them in parallel, the voltage stays the same—12v—but the amps add up, so now you have 1,000Ah. So what you need is to place ten 100Ah 12V deep-cycle batteries in parallel to get what you want.

Lead Acid or Lithium

There are at least three schools of thought when it comes to making a decision on the type of battery that you need. You've already figured out the capacity, but the kind of battery is important because it speaks directly to safety, durability, and reliability. It really comes down to whom you speak to. Some old-timers will swear by the lead acid, but the newer guys will tell you that the LiFePO4 batteries are superior. We will give you a balanced view here, and in time as you do more RV-ing or sailing, you will get to a point where you will have your own preferences as well.

Before we get into the qualitative issues between the choices, the one point that you should know is that the lead acid batteries are very different in their charge profiles and in their discharge profiles. Let's do the simple one first. The lithium can be charged in one go; you can bulk charge it from 0% to 100% without interruption and even use the batteries while they are being charged. That's the easy part. On the other hand, in lead acid batteries, you have to charge them in stages. They require three profiles for charging, to be specific, each requiring a lower charge current. The first round is bulk-charging that takes you from 0% to 80%, then from 81% to 95% with absorption charging, and then for the last 5%, you have to float charge it. That alone alters the time it takes to fully charge a bank of lead acid batteries. The amount of time it takes to charge has consequences on your efficiency and the cost—if you need to increase the battery bank and solar panels to account for delayed charging.

Weight

Let's start with weight issues. Lead acid batteries are heavy. If you have to pile on ten of these, you will be placing a huge weight burden on your vehicle. In comparison, lithium batteries weigh approximately a third of lead acids, while holding similar power capacity. Take, for instance, a bank of lead acid batteries tied to provide 300Ah. They would come in at a whopping 400 pounds. 900Ah would be over 1,200 pounds. On the other hand, a bank of lithium batteries with the same capacity would come in at just under 150 pounds. Think about that in terms of weight to benefit. If you have a small RV, it would exceed the hitch weight, and if you place it in the back, it's going to destabilize your set up.

Size

Comparing lead acid batteries to lithium batteries, you will find that they are also vastly different in size. Lithium batteries are much smaller and can fit into spaces that similar-capacity leads won't be able to fit into.

Lifespan

When you think about costs as part of your checklists of considerations, you inadvertently have to think about lifespan. The shorter the lifespan, the more often you have to replace something. I look at the cost per day as a good metric for myself or in terms of batteries, cost per cycle. That way, I feel like I amortize the cost of purchase, maintenance, and installation over the item's lifetime. When I apply this rationale to batteries, it becomes clear that lithium batteries come out way ahead. A fairly priced lithium will last about 5,000 cycles, whereas a good lead acid will only be good for between 400 and 500 cycles. A cycle is a full charge and a full discharge. So let's say I pay $1,000 for a bank of lithiums and $700 for a bank of leads, putting all other issues, of size, weight, maintenance issues, and discharge efficiency, each cycle amortizes to 20 cents for the lithium ($1,000/5,000 cycles), whereas the lead amortizes to $1.4 per cycle ($700/500). This is just an illustration to contrast the dollars-per-cycle argument.

When you take this into consideration, you have to take one more element into consideration and that is discharge efficiency, which is covered later in this chapter.

Venting

To some, this may not be an issue, but to many, this is. When it comes to lead acid batteries, you need to vent them and make sure they vent to the outside. These batteries vent both when they are charged and when they are being used. The fumes are toxic and acidic so you want to be able to release them in a way that it doesn't find its way back into the interior or to others nearby when parked. It is a requirement that the batteries are placed externally. On the other hand, lithium batteries do not vent any fumes whatsoever and can be placed internally or in a compartment that is accessible from the inside. If you ever have to go out to the battery in the midst of winter where you are parked and fiddle around with the battery from the outside, you will instantly realize how this is not the best way to do things.

Maintenance

Lithium batteries do not require any maintenance. There is no electrolyte to top up or terminals to clean. Lead acids, on the other hand, are notorious when it comes to maintenance issues. The first one is the periodic cleaning for the terminals that oxidize. The second is the constant need to top up the electrolyte.

Discharge Efficiency

There is one thing that most people do not realize and that is the fact that the appliances that go into the RV, boat, or van add up to be an expensive piece of the puzzle. One of the things that reduce their lifespan is the fluctuation in voltage that could occur when using lead acid batteries. The lead batteries are notorious for voltage reduction as the batteries drain out. It's like what happens when your AA battery starts to get low and the flashlight dims because of it. That diminishes because the voltage has dropped toward the end of the cycle and if that happens on a daily basis, the appliances—many of which have sensitive chips and motherboards—start to degrade in performance. It is not worth it. Lithium batteries, on the other hand, have stable voltage all the way to the last packet of energy. Speaking of efficiency, lead acid batteries only store 75% of the amps that are sent to them. As such, if your solar panel is sending them 10 amps, your battery is only storing 7.5 amps. In lithium batteries, the efficiency is 99%, so if you send 10 amps to the lithium batteries, they will store 9.9 amps. This translates to dollars as well. It means that you would need to get a larger solar array to charge the batteries at the same rate as the lithium batteries.

While we are on this subject, you should also know about something called a C rating. Most deep cycle batteries have a C rating of 20. Most calculations are also based on that. What it tells you is that the battery is ideally designed to discharge at a certain rate over a 20-hour period. Take, for instance, a 100Ah deep cycle battery. If unsaid, then you can assume that it is C20. That means, it will discharge over 20 hours. If you have 100Ah then divide it by 20 hours, what you have is 5 amps. That means the battery is designed to discharge at a peak of 5 amps. But since you will be hooking these batteries up in parallel, you will be able to add them up. What you have if you had 400Ah across four batteries is 20 amp-per-hour peak discharge. If you look back at my illustration where I had 990 amp-hours across 10 batteries (100Ah per battery), then I have 50-amp peak usage.

Cost Advantages

Just about the only place where lead acids seem to win is when it comes to upfront costs. Amp to amp, the lead acid is about a quarter of the price. A 100Ah lead acid costs about $200, while a lithium battery costs about $800. The price will vary tremendously depending on where you buy them from and what bells and whistles come with the battery.

When you are trying to set up a 12V 600Ah system that can translate to between $5,000 for lithium batteries versus $1,200 for lead acid batteries; I get that it can be very expensive when you have just put together all the appliances that are going into a new build—not to mention the cost of the rig itself. But the thing that you should think about is the long-term cost. We have already seen what weight can do, and we have seen how it can affect total weight and the balance of the rig; imagine putting six lead acid batteries that total up 400 pounds.

The other thing that you have to consider is the usable cycles. 5,000 cycles on a system that costs $5,000 works out to be $1 per cycle. But $1,2oo for 500 cycles is $2.40 per cycle. My thought on this matter is fairly straightforward, and is kind of like what came first: the chicken or the egg? Plan on what you are going to install in terms of appliances and plan for the slightly larger load. Then get the capacity in your solar system and batteries to match that—spend the money here first then with what is left, get the appliances. You will, of course, come up a little short, but you can put off some of the appliances to later. When the time comes to install these, your rig will already have the capacity to handle it, and it will all come together nicely. If, instead, you spend your money on the appliances and have an insufficient amount for the system, you will end up compromising on quality, because you'll be trying to cut down on costs. That's when it becomes tempting to use lead acid batteries. Trust me, it will ruin the experience. The other kind of RVer decides to split the difference. Install adequate capacity for a slightly reduced appliance list with the view to expand both later. You don't want to do this either, because what will happen is that you will have to reconfigure the system and then pull some stuff out, and it gets complicated. You will end up spending more. If you want to save in the long term, get the infrastructure to the point that you want it to be at then slowly lay in the amenities. That way, it is always a clean build from the ground up.

As far as brands are concerned, I shall leave you to have some fun with the shopping process. My suggestion is that you read the reviews carefully on the brands that are available and speak to a salesman to get a good picture and to build a rapport so that he can help in the event you need to go back to him—unless of course you buy them online, and they have stellar customer service.

Chapter 4: How to Select your Components

Let's get a quick overview of the solar infrastructure in a remote platform. Sunlight hits the solar panel, and from there current leaves the panel. At this point, it is DC current. That then goes to a charge controller and then on to the power bank, which is a string of batteries arranged in parallel formation. Since not all your equipment is going to run on DC, you need an inverter to convert DC to AC. At this point, you now have AC and DC power at the wall. Many of the appliances you buy will need AC, so along with the list of things that you have planned, a diagram of where they will be installed is a good idea so you know what electricity to channel to that location.

Now that you have the heart of your system set aside, it is time to look at how to choose your other components, including the solar panels, the charge controller, and the inverter. We will also look at choosing wires and generators for back up. The information is sufficient to get you on your way, but if you want more detail, you can refer to my other book, *Solar Power: Making the Smart Switch to Solar Power—And Staying Within Budget!*

As with all things, there is a balance one has to strike when making a large-ticket purchase. There are numerous brands with multiple features for each of the compliments that we discuss in this section.

Selecting Solar Panels

There are two things you need to do to select solar panels. One is quantitative, the other is qualitative. The quantitative aspects are like how you calculated your power bank capacity.

There are three types of solar panels out there. Each of them has different cost-, utility-, and longevity-profiles. You have to choose what's best for you. It is not always certain that the most expensive is the best for you in the same way that the cheapest is not always the most cost-effective. You need to look at the entire picture and see which ones give you the best return for your investment.

The basic element of a solar panel is silicon (not silicone). Silicon is represented by "Si" on the periodic table. It is basically what computer chips are made of, and it is the constituent of beach sand in its oxide form. It is an abundant element on the planet and has multiple electrical uses, one of which is solar cells.

The three types of solar panels are monocrystalline, polycrystalline, and amorphous (or also known as thin film). Each kind has varying qualities and is not easily classified as best or worst. They are just different and built for different users with different budgets in mind.

There is a funny thing about these silicon structures that we need to look at—efficiency. Efficiency comes in many forms. When it comes to silicon panel efficiency, it is a little different. The most efficient silicon happens to be one that has to go through highly expensive purification processes. It gets to a point that the most effective silicon panel is highly effective, but the economics of it makes it unfeasible for over 90% of the market. As such, when it comes to efficiency in silicon panels, we have to look beyond the purification process and see which of the three kinds makes sense for the way we are going to make use of it. Instead, the efficiency is not about purity, it is about cost and space. In other words, you need to look at downstream efficiency instead of upstream efficiency. In terms of downstream efficiency, we come to mono-, poly-, and amorphous crystalline structures.

It is pretty simple to distinguish one from the other. It's a pretty good bet that you have seen at least one, if not all, of them. The monocrystalline panels are the ones that you see that look like the corners have been cut off. In one panel, you have individual squares with their corner cut off, so if you look at the whole panel, it consists of a number of these arranged in rows and columns. The polycrystalline solar panels are visually distinguishable from their monocrystalline cousins. The entre panel is uniformly arranged so that it looks like a dark blue screen without the diamond-shaped tie structure that you see in the mono panels. Finally, the amorphous thin film is also distinguishable from the other two, because they are manufactured differently and placed on a substrate that can be either hard (like glass) or on something flexible that can be rolled.

Among the three, monocrystalline has the best efficiency (15% to 22%) and made from the highest grade of silicon, making them the most expensive in dollar terms. Because of their efficiency, you need smaller panels to get the same output as comparable panels made from poly or amorphous silicon. If you were to compare them side-by-side with amorphous panels, they would produce almost 400% greater output. Most manufacturers put a 25-year warranty on them, because these panels can last that long. When you think of costs, you should amortize them to get a true reflection of your expense. Something that costs twice as much but lasts four times as long is certainly a better bet. But the thing to note here is that there are two downsides. One is obviously the cost—the initial outlay can be expensive. But, more importantly, the second downside is the nature of the electricity generation profile. Monocrystalline panels have a warm temperature range that produces at optimal levels. If it gets too hot, then the electricity generation starts to degrade. If you think that you will be out in summer on most holidays, or you will be in hot climates and want to run an above-roof air-conditioning unit, then maybe monos are not a good idea.

On the one hand, thin film, or amorphous solar panels, is easily produced and cheaper than the other two kinds. They are significantly less efficient—with efficiency in the 4% to 8% range as opposed to mono, which comes in at more than 20%. But they cost significantly less, even after you consider you need five times the square footage compared to mono. The limiting factor is not so much the price, but whether you will be using it in hot temperatures. Thin film is impervious to excessive temperatures. You are also limited by the footprint—in this case, how much space you have on the roof of your RV or van.

When you pick a solar panel, calculate the square footage you have available and balance it with the power users that you hope to have. This is a zero-sum game. You can have an infinite amount of solar panels available to drive all the appliances you need. You will have to cut back on the appliances and power usage or get a bigger vehicle to supplement it.

Selecting a solar charge controller

You need to use a solar charge controller to prevent your batteries from overcharging or over-discharging. There are times that your solar panels may charge the batteries more than you had planned for (like when you drive on a sunny day in snow-covered areas) and that extra current from the panels will degrade the batteries. To prevent that, you need to get a solar charge controller.

There are only two things you need to know to be able to make a selection. First, you need to know what voltage your system is designed for, is it 12, 24, or 48 volts? In this book, we have been looking at 12-volt systems. So, if you followed everything here, it would be a 12-volt charge controller. There are some controllers that auto-detect the voltage and adjust accordingly.

The second is the current that you will be looking at during peak charging. For this, you need to look at the solar panels you are purchasing. They will list peak charging in their manual. Look for what is called "short circuit current." Once you get that number, add a buffer to it. Let's say your panel's short circuit current is 8 amps; if you add a 25% buffer, that means you need to get a 10-amp solar charge controller.

Selecting an inverter

The next thing you need to get is an inverter. You need one specifically for RVs, boats, and vans. They have ones that go in home PV setups, but you want to make sure you tell your salesman that you are putting this in an RV. The next thing is that your inverter has to work during two phases of use. The first is when you start something heavy, like an air-conditioning unit or a pump. That initial startup causes a surge and the peak demand is high, but only for a short time, then it reverts back to a stable consumption pattern. So you need to get an idea—and you can do this based on your list that we made in the earlier part of the book with all the appliances and the power usage. Remember that an inverter is there specifically for you to be able to run all your appliances that have AC because the current coming from your batteries is all DC. Once you get the peak rating, the next is that you have to figure out the typical rating. The typical rating is the load that you will place on it in most cases. This is the load that will come after the pumps start up or the air-conditioning starts up. Once the momentary peaks are hit, the typical current consumption is what you need to calculate to get this number.

Selecting wire

Selecting the right wire is something that most people take for granted when setting up their system—be it their PV system at home or on their boat, or even their hi-fi stereo. What they do not realize is that wiring is one of the most common ways to improve efficiency and to create a better overall PV system. The wrong wiring can not only reduce the efficiency of your system but could damage your appliance, or worse, be a fire hazard.

A good way to start is to have a diagram of your setup and then locate where your battery bank is going to be located. You need to look at the capacity of the solar panels and the distance the cables going from the solar array to the solar charge controller, and then the wiring that goes from there to the batteries. You also need cables to tie the batteries in a parallel arrangement. Afterward, measure the cables for DC power to the outlets that you think will have DC power, and then connect cables to go from the batteries to the inverter. From there again, you need to have wiring that goes from there to the outlets. The way that you get the wiring right is to calculate the peak and typical loads on each cable. So, for instance, the wiring that goes from the inverter to the outlet that powers the 15,000BTU air-conditioning unit needs to be a lower gauge (thicker wire) so that the resistance of the wire is lower and the required amps are delivered to the unit. Wires can be expensive, so optimize the lengths to the outlets that you need.

Selecting bank voltage monitors/power meters

A battery monitor is an important part of the setup even though it is frequently misunderstood and not noticed. There are two things that the monitor does. One, it gives you a readout of the current state of your batteries, and two, it allows you to plan ahead to charge or discharge your battery. In most cases, battery monitors are not just a voltage monitor. Voltage monitors are a good indicator of the state of the battery. It is very common that batteries will start to fade in voltage as they come to the limit of their useful charge. The moment the voltage starts to back off, you know that it is time to get it charged. Many of the monitors today can be connected to a computer module that automatically runs the software to get your solar panels working and charging your system. Choose one that is able to hook up to a computer or get a readout directly on your smartphone via an app. In fact, if you can, you should be able to tie up all the individual parts of the PV system to an app that will allow you to control your RV remotely.

Selecting backup power

Backup power is not absolutely necessary. It depends on your profile—how you travel, where you go, and how often you stop at a marina for boats or at a place with electricity in the case of an RV. On the other hand, if you are planning to boondock, then you will need to have a generator for those times when the sun is not shining as bright or you used more than you intended to. Backup power is typically a generator. We will look at how we can choose a generator and what we need to look for when choosing a generator.

There are three kinds of generators to choose from: diesel, gasoline, and liquid propane. If you are concerned about burning clean, then your first option would be liquid propane, followed by diesel, and lastly gasoline. But gasoline is easily available anywhere and everywhere. You can fill it up when you fill up your RV. Diesel is the next easily available and followed by propane that is not as easy to find. That is the second thing you want to think about: If you are the kind that keeps a generator just to back up for times when there is no sunlight and your use would be rare. Just remember that propane produces about 91,500BTU per gallon while gasoline produces over 125,000BTU per gallon. But gasoline can't be stored over long periods. They degrade and the fumes can build up to dangerous levels. Propane, on the other hand, can be stored indefinitely. If, as we mentioned earlier, you rarely use the generator, then propane would be a better way to go. If you turn on your generators often, then gasoline would be a better choice. Once you decide on this, the next is the fact that generators are not all made the same. If you want a portable generator just to run a pump, that's one thing. But if you want a generator for your RV, boat, or van, there are generators designed specifically for that.

An RV-class generator is what you need to look for. I am not aware of a rule, regulation, or law that says you have to get an RV generator for your vehicle, but it is a good way to go for a number of reasons. Specifically, because it has higher horsepower and is designed to be stowed as part of the RV with the proper venting all designed into it.

Just like the inverters, generators also have two ratings that you will want to keep in mind: the startup, or peak power, and the typical, or constant power. In generator terms, they're called startup wattage and running wattage. If you take a 30,00-watt generator, you can't assume that it has 3,000 watts of continuous running wattage—it's going to be startup wattage. That means it can give you a burst of 3,000 watts, but that is unsustainable for more than 10 or 15 minutes. To get an idea of what the running wattage is, you need to check the manual.

The next thing to determine when looking to buy a generator is noise output. You do not want to be a nuisance to yourself or your neighbors. The last thing anyone wants to hear after they've left a noisy city behind and come into nature is a loud generator pumping out noise and exhaust. Many campgrounds limit the noise to 60 decibels at 50 feet. Make sure you look for something that is at least at that level or better.

Another thing to consider is whether the generators are permanent or portable. Usually, if you have a large RV, then you are looking for a permanent fixture that is housed in a compartment that can be soundproofed and the exhaust can be ventilated up to the roof of the RV. If it is something portable, they are typically lighter and you can move them around. It comes in handy when you can store them in the cabin and then place them outside when running them.

Finally, there is the issue that can be the most important of all—whether or not you can place them in parallel. Placing them in parallel allows you to place the generator between your battery and your solar panels. When you can place them in parallel, you can charge your batteries when there isn't enough sunlight to get your batteries to power up. If you can place them in parallel, then you can wire them in a way where you can switch power sources from batteries to a generator. The wiring for this is different.

In the first instance, when you place the generator in parallel with the batteries, your batteries go to the inverter and you get power from there at all times. The benefit of this is the simpler wiring, and it's a neat package. But if the batteries short-out or are spoilt in any way, you will not be able to get power from your generators to your inverter without doing some rewiring. If you get good batteries, then this is not going to be a problem. You can also have a mechanical switch that moves the power directly to the circuit breakers and then on to the outlets, but that would end up costing more.

It all comes down to the kind of RV you have and the kind of RVing you will be doing. Either way, a generator as a backup is always a good idea. It will give you the freedom to extend your reach from civilization for longer periods, and it will serve as a peace of mind for those times when you don't have enough sunlight to get a good charge.

Solar array disconnect switch

There are two kinds of disconnect switches found in the market. You only need one of them. The other is for stationary systems that connect to the grid. The first is the solar array DC disconnect. This is the one you need. This is the one that allows you to disengage the power coming from the solar array and going to the solar charge controller. You want to have this so that on days that you are not traveling or charging, the panels aren't continuously sending current to the batteries.

Now that you know that you need one of these, the next question is what you need to look for when planning for one. First off, it is not as simple as just placing a rocker switch between the array and the controller. You have to be cognizant of the fact that this is DC power, and DC is prone to arcing if you are not using something that is designed for it. As long as there is sunlight outside, the panels are going to be sending DC down the wiring, and if it is a rocker switch that is installed, flicking it off to open the circuit could cause a sustained arc. That, if mixed with fumes, could be an ignition that is unintended.

Fuses for your wiring

Why do you need fuses for your PV system in your RV or your boat? The simple answer is that there are rare periods when there is a chance that the wires heat up due to spikes in current, a malfunction in the appliance, or even a short in the wiring due to rodents, perhaps. But when there is a spike and the wires get too hot, they act as a heating filament and a source of ignition. They may be the smallest component of the entire system, but they are undoubtedly the most important when it comes to a mishap.

The first thing you need to remember is that it is not just the amperage of the solar panels, but also how you tie them together. If you tie them in parallel, your voltage may be the same but your amps are additive. So if you have 5 amps coming from the first panel, by the time you get to the third panel, the wiring is carrying 15 amps. You need to take this into account when you wire the panels and select the right gauge and the right fuse. If you place a 12-amp fuse on the first segment, that will work, but if you place a 12-amp fuse in the second segment, then that fuse is going to break. One way to do this is to place 12-amp fuses on the solar panel prior to the combiner, and then use a thicker wire to tie them together. If you place them in series, then you will not have this issue.

In the same way, place a fuse after the combiner, after the controller, and after the inverter. Use a 25% rule of thumb above the short circuit current, and fuse each junction. This keeps the entire system safe.

Chapter 5: How to Install Your Own Solar Panels

Now we come to the point where we have all the equipment planned and have all their specs. We want to put them together virtually. Never buy the stuff until you have exhaustively planned everything out. If you want to really have some fun with it, you can even do a mock-up of it with all the equipment after you purchase them to see if it all works. If it all works, then you can start the installation process in the RV. As you can see, this takes quite a bit of planning. It is also an iterative process, and you should bring lots of patience to the table.

Can my roof handle it?

The first thing we are going to look at is if your roof can handle the weight of the solar panels that you are planning on installing. If you end up having a heavier solar panel—in the event you want to have a frame in order to angle the panels—the weight could start to add up quickly. If you add some kind of a motor to remotely raise the panels into an incline, then that will increase the weight even more. Don't forget that you may also have planned on a rooftop box air-conditioning unit, and that will take up space as well. Most RV owners forget this part of it and may be frustrated when the time comes to install the panels and the framework. Check with your RV manufacturer what weight and where the mounting points are for the roof. If you need to go above that, then you need to get the frame and the roof fortified by adding crossbars or steel frames.

Keep in mind, though, that will raise the weight of the RV. Make sure that the axels can handle it, and that the tow is rated for the additional weight.

Installing Solar Panels

Once you have your solar panels, there are a number of ways that you can get them installed onto your roof with the least amount of risk of damage to the roof, and the highest assurance that they aren't going to get blown off in the wind the moment the speedometer hits 60 mp/h (or 100 km/h for us metric folks).

The best way to do this is to line up your solar panels and lay them down width-wise so that they line up next to each other.

1. Use heavy duty aluminum rails and lay then parallel on the ground

2. Use shorter aluminum rails as crossbeams and use two crossbeams for every three feet of length. (Let's say you have a ten foot run from the front of the RV to the rear then you will have ten feet of aluminum rails going from front to back. The cross beam will go perpendicular to this and will be placed no more than 3 feet apart, in this case since you have a ten foot run, use for cross beams at equal spacing of 2.5 feet.)

3. The cross beams should extend from the base of the solar panel by at least 6 inches. This is to hinge it to the roof of the RV. In this example, there will be four hinges. When you plant the hinges on the roof, make sure to use a vulcanized rubber/silicone bushing to serve as a sealant for the holes and to keep the vibrations to a minimum.

4. Attach the panels to the long beams and run the wiring in a flexible conduit. Anchor that conduit to the rails. Remember, while you are cozy in the driver's seat driving to your favorite destination, the cables and solar panels are going to be subjected to 60 mph winds. Everything here needs to be anchored down.

5. Place two locking mechanism on the opposite side of the hinged rails and lock those down when you are on the road.

6. Bring the wires down to the junction box where the fuses will be located (more on this in the next section.)

Batteries

Once you have installed the PV panels and wired them to the combiner and the fuses, your next step is to pick a location in the RV for the batteries. You can do this when you have chosen your batteries on paper. The two things you need to watch are the dimensions and the weight of the power bank. From here, you can figure out where to place the batteries—different RV designs have different places already meant for batteries. Some even come with ventilation in case you are using lead acid batteries.

Step-by-step general instructions to install your batteries

1. Before installing them, follow the manufacturer's guide to setting up your batteries. Remove packaging and protective coverings as instructed.

2. Place the battery in the location that you have determined. If there are ties in the RV, you can tie them down, or you can use 2x4s to form a barrier and anchor the 2x4s to the chassis and then tie the batteries to the 2x4s. Make sure the batteries are stable and do not have space to rock or slide. They should also not be able to hop either, in case you hit a bump. For this, place a 2x4 on the batteries to anchor those down as well.

3. Tie the terminals in parallel or series the way you had planned to.

4. Run the wires (after calculating the proper gauge) from the common line leading to the fuse box that leads to the solar charge controller.

5. Then, connect the wires leaving the batteries to the fuse box that will lead to the inverter and the DC outlets.

6. Make sure that you insulate all the wires and anchor them to a stable surface. Never leave your wires in a bunch, and do not leave them hanging.

Step-by-step general instructions to install your charge controllers

1. The charge controller comes between the solar panel array and the battery

2. Find a suitable location in the RV that is easily accessible and have a box that you can close and latch. Run the wires from the combiner to this box and place the fuse box here.

3. Install the solar charge control downstream from the fuses.

4. Run the cables from the battery bank atop this box, place the fuses that come prior to the battery here, and connect the battery cables here. It will also be where you will connect the generator leads later.

5. Run the wires from the controller to the battery fuses.

Step-by-step general instructions to install your inverter

1. Install a junction box like you did for the charge controller, but this time install this close to your power bank. You can even install this down in the battery compartment.

2. In the box, secure the inverter and attach it to a fuse box. Each fuse goes to a line that leads into the RV's cabin and to the different locations planned for a specific appliance.

3. Use a wire gauge that the manufacturer recommends or one that is larger.

4. Secure the connections and make certain that there is no possibility of loose wires detaching from the connections. You want to prevent arcing at all costs.

5. Next, connect the wiring to the fuse box that goes to the batteries.

At this point, you need to place the power monitors in the cabin and wire them as instructed in the manual. You should have all the wires tied in at this point, and make sure that the disconnect switch is open—meaning that the panels aren't supplying current to the batteries. Check each connection with an amp meter to make sure that there is flow.

A point to note is that all wires need to be connected and insulated. Keep all points of connection dry, and make sure they will not come into contact with water or have the risk of being jarred loose.

Conclusion

A good way to categorize your wiring is to keep them in zones. This will allow you to troubleshoot inoperative components when the time comes. Designing electrical systems is about emergent situations. Everything that you do when you design and install them is about keeping it safe in case of a fault. Never design your system thinking that it will be faultless.

PV systems are designed to cater to most of your power needs, but they may not be able to take on all of it. You will have to supplement it in one way or another. If you have to park at a campground with services, then you can get your batteries charged there or you can have a generator that supplements the power you need.

The best way to get the PV system to operate efficiently when you are parked is to make sure that you are in the best angle possible for the sun to give you the most light. This is the reason some campers have adjustable inclines for the panel. If you want to get really fancy, you can place the panels on a frame that changes angles using a sensor that tracks the sun and then raises or lowers the inclination to point to the sun. But in most cases, that only works out to be half the picture, because it only has one set of hinges. Once you reach maximum inclination at midday, it's time for you to re-park your vehicle. Say, for instance, if you are parked facing the north and your panels are hinged on the right, then in the morning, the panels will be at a full upright position to take advantage of the morning sun. As the day progresses, the angle will reduce until it is flat on your roof at midday. At this point, it no longer has the ability to cross over. You will have to re-park your RV to face south, and your sensors will slowly adjust the inclination to catch the sun as it starts its descent to the western horizon. If you don't have this tracker, then a manual inclination can allow you to park your van facing west (assuming you are in the northern hemisphere), and then tilt the frame toward the sun in the south and leave it that way all day and just reposition the van as it starts to set in the west.

The best way for you to get the most out of your solar system is to keep the panels clean and to make sure that the wirings are always snug. Every week, do a walk-around and inspect your equipment to look for degradation, rust, snug fit, cuts, tears, and anything that shouldn't be there. Make it a point to inspect your battery compartment and make sure there are no critters nesting in there or any fluids leaking. If you have a gasoline generator and hardly use it, run the generator during your inspection days. Don't let fuel stay in there and degrade. Also, make sure that all the wiring to the generators are in good order.

Above and beyond that, you should send your RV to a maintenance shop to inspect and fix things, or you can do it yourself once a year. Replace wiring that you think needs it, change housing and protective covers, and grease the hinges to panels and frames.

RVing with PV is a great way to untether yourself from the trappings of a stationary world. Getting closer to nature and finding your peace is all tied to how well you can make it comfortable in the RV, and how easy and hassle-free you make power generation. As time passes, you will see that your comfort and peace are closely tied to how efficient your power system is, and that is the reason you want to look for quality systems instead of cheap systems.

I hope you found this informative. Happy boondocking!

Like the book? The greatest compliment is leaving a review on Amazon. Thanks in advance ☺

Solar Power

How To Harness The Sun To Power Your Life – And Go Off-Grid While Doing It

Mike Holsworth

Table of Contents

Chapter 5: How Much Does It Cost and Where Do I Buy It?

Basic solar system elements

Value of a reliable manufacturer

Different Types of Panels

2. Polycrystalline
3. Thin-film
4. Concentrated PV cell

Chapter 6: How Do I Know Where To Put My Panels?

a. The roof's condition
b. Direction
c. Angle
d. Distance between panels
e. Temperature
f. Shading
g. Dirt and dust
h. Irradiance
i. Snow

Chapter 7: How To Set Up Superior Solar Power Systems For Energy Efficiency?

1. Introduction
2. DIY Project
4. Step-By-Step Installation: Off-Grid PV System
5. Tips to Hire A Professional

Chapter 8: Moving Off The Grid

a. How much energy do I need?

b. Can my excess energy flow BACK to the grid if I want?

c. What is the BENEFIT of doing this? How much can the average household save?

Chapter 1: What is Solar Power?

The term solar power conjures images of big panels and glass-like fixtures. These arrangements are technically known as solar panels. TV documentaries and advertisements usually show large frames on rooftops. These panels are made up of PV or photovoltaic cells (for capturing solar energy or the sun's light and heat). The whole set-up is designed to convert sunlight into electricity (for home use).

Terminology

Electric Supply

Home appliances are made up of electric and electronic components or parts. Your TV, fridge, air conditioner, computers, lights, basically everything in your home requires electricity. The electrical wires supply this current typically from the mains. There are switchboards, plugs, and switches that control current passage through cables. Technically, this set-up is known as alternating current or AC. The home, flat or apartment receives this electricity from power lines located on the street. The power company transmits voltage to houses or shops over these public wires or lines (also known as a grid system).

The companies store excessive amounts of electrical energy in a power station. They have computers and large-sized electrical/electronic parts to control the power supply. The fundamental difference between energy and power is that the former is stored, while the latter is in action. Since all this equipment has to be maintained, power companies charge the customers. They set up meters to read the amount of power that is utilized by each house. The consumers have to pay the electricity bills based on these accurate meter readings.

Anyone who has used a digital clock, TV or video game remote would have seen a battery. These cells or batteries supply direct current or DC. They convert chemical energy into small amounts of electrical energy. This is sufficient to use a remote or keep the clock ticking; however, once the stored energy runs out entirely, consider replacing the cells.

Solar Panels

The light from the sun is also one form of energy - known as solar energy. Just like the chemical energy, it too can be converted into electricity. For this purpose, large solar panels have to be fixed on the roof of a house. These panels have photovoltaic or PV cells - for converting photons (light) into voltages (power). The more significant the number of panels, the higher the amount of generated electricity. Of course, the sun too should be shining brightly.

- Solar Power is the active energy (electricity), which the sunlight generates.
- A panel system is fixed on the roof to convert light into power.
- PV cells, electrical circuits, and charge controllers achieve the conversion.
- The large-sized batteries (DC form) stores the converted solar energy.
- An electronic device, known as the inverter, is used to convert DC into AC.
- This AC power is used to power your home.

- A well-designed solar power system also has various vital parts.
- They are the meter, connectors, cables, junction boxes, and cabinets (for battery/inverter).
- The entire system is also carefully grounded to prevent shocks or accidents.
- The earth or ground under our feet is a good conductor of electricity.

Grid-connected system.

If the sun is too bright and hot, then a lot of solar power is generated, but the system is set up to store only fixed amounts of energy. Excess energy can be sent to the power station through the grid; however, homeowners have to contact the power company first. They have to work together and fix additional circuits. These extra cables establish a grid connection and take away excess energy to the power station.

On the other hand, there are rainy days without any sunshine. There is no solar power supply from the panels on these days. You will have to depend on the regular power supply from the company. Whether you are on or off the grid, you will need to pay the electricity bills. The meters are a crucial component in home electricity supply. Digitized meters record the amount of electricity spent in a month. The customer receives the statement, and he or she has to pay without any delays.

The solar panel system that is on the grid is more efficient. The homeowner can set up a system to switch between regular and solar power supplies. The main power grid receives the excess energy, which is also metered. The electric company provides a credit on the bill if there is surplus. The exact retail charges depend upon the local tariff and other regulations. All in all, the customers do benefit as solar power is a clean and green source.

How To Install A Solar Power System

First, choose the most efficient PV panels for your home and region. Take various factors like sunlight, roof area, and energy needs into consideration. Remember that an expensive model is also durable and more effective as they capture a higher amount of sunlight and resist wear and tear. The additional components like battery, charge controller, wiring, and inverter should also be of high quality.

- First, you have to calculate average energy needs and make the purchases.
- Those with a scientific understanding can do some first-hand research.
- You may want to take help of a professional solar power system company.
- The PV panels have to be selected by wattage, voltage, and size.
- Larger panels are useful if the roof area is not very spacious or large.
- Position the glass mirrors at an angle of 90 degrees to the sun.
- Choose between the north or the south direction (depending on hemisphere), or whichever direction is brighter due to sunlight.
- Make sure there are no sunlight obstructions like trees or walls.
- Connect the solar array of panels for generating the maximum current.

- Wiring usually runs from panels to batteries through a charge controller.
- Connections are also fixed between inverter, battery, and main power supply.
- Grounding is also necessary to protect the equipment from lightning or power surge.
- There are various methods for setting up the solar power panel system.
- The configurations also vary for business offices, homes, stores, garages, and RV's.
- Safety is paramount, and professionals are best equipped to install a PV system.
- The solar power system also has combiner box (for wiring) and surge protection.

Components

Let us look at all the elements or parts of the PV solar power installation:

- Solar photovoltaic modules

- Array mounting racks
- Battery
- The battery bank with cabling and housing structure
- Charge controller
- Battery disconnect
- Grounding equipment
- Combiner box with surge protection
- Inverter
- Meters – system meter and kilowatt-hour meter
- Disconnects
- Array DC disconnect
- Inverter DC disconnect
- Inverter AC disconnect
- Exterior AC disconnect

Installation Guidelines

It is recommended that the homeowner purchases all the components mentioned above versus making them yourself. Be sure to follow the regional laws and install a risk-free system. The following instructions are useful in determining the success or failure of a PV system installation:

A. Personnel

- Team effort is more suitable for full installations as they are complicated.
- Solar company, electrical sub-contractor or electrician can be contacted.
- Company experts have more experience in PV systems compared to others.
- The team has to co-ordinate their services and install as per building codes.
- Solar power systems require inspections, meetings, and warranty assurance.

B. Standards of Safety

- Anything that has electricity and high voltages has to be safe.
- The installing team should protect the equipment, residents, and the property at all costs.
- The solar panels and circuits are categorized as an electrical system.
- The PV panel set-up has to satisfy electrical safety codes for your applicable area.
- During the installation, one should assure the health and safety of all personnel.
- Eliminate the electrical hazards and risks associated with climbing high roofs.
- The installation experts should follow the best practices for their safety.

C. Wiring Rules

- Direct current (DC) wiring panel fixtures are

usually very large sized.

- The installing company should focus on protecting outdoor wiring against high temperatures, wind, and rain.
- One can drill the roofs for conduits, cabling, and electrical wiring.
- Make sure the roofs are sealed off with the help of construction experts.

D. System Design

- One can install an pre-engineered panel system based off their needs
- Carefully size the various parts for setting up a perfect PV system.
- The building's features like shade, roof angle, gable, etc., has to be considered.
- Design the off-grid and grid-connected systems with precision.
- Solar companies, traders, and distributors can also plan and implement.

E. Costs

- One can use software tools for design and cost estimation.
- One can calculate the installation costs in "per watt" terms of energy.
- Efficiency and cost are inversely related to each other in PV panels.
- Labor charges depend on the complexity of the task (e.g. roof type and building layout).
- If the solar power system uses all the components, the cost increases.

Chapter 2: How Does It Work?

Energy

In physical sciences, energy is measured as the capacity to do work. It has to be produced, stored, transmitted, and spent on useful work. The two main types of energy are potential (stored) and kinetic (work). Chemical, mechanical, gravitational, and nuclear power are stored as potential energies, while electricity, heat, motion, and sound are kinetic energies that carry out useful work.

Power is defined as the rate of work execution or amount of energy spent in unit time (seconds, minutes, and hours, etc.). Electricity is a specific type of energy, and it has many sources; they include hydro power (water and dams), nonrenewable sources (burning coal), and thermonuclear (radioactive reactions) energy. Some alternative sources of power are windmills (air), biomass (burning wood), tidal power (ocean waves), and solar panels (sunlight).

Energy is measured in a unit known as joules. 1 Joule is equivalent to 1 watt per second. Power companies measure electricity consumption in a kilowatt-hour (kWh). 1 kWh is equivalent to 3.6×106 J (3600 kJ or 3.6 MJ). Electricity usage is also calculated in units of kilowatt-hours per year (kWh/yr).

How Do Solar Panel Systems Work?

The solar panel company installs the power system using insulated wiring. Every modern home has the main power supply from the grid. The panel system is set up, and the electrical cables connect various components to form a circuit. Electricity is electron charges running through this circuitry. Electricity powers the multiple appliances without any interruption. Batteries, inverters, and generators assure a glitch-free 24-7-power supply.

Let us look at how the solar panel system functions to generate sufficient power:

- First, light from the sun directly strikes the PV panels on the roof.

- Panels are made up of individual solar cells (inter-connected for specific voltages).
- Solar cells capture this sunlight and convert it into direct current (DC).
- Electrical circuits (wires and controllers) carry this DC into large-sized batteries.
- This stored solar energy is converted from DC into AC by an inverter.
- The wires or circuits from the inverter enter the home's main lines.
- They supply solar power (in converted form - AC) to bulbs, TVs, fridges, etc.
- The generated and stored energy is measured in volts and amps.
- Home appliances are rated in watts, watt-hour, amps, and amp-hour.
- Energy or power that is stored/generated or spent in an hour is a useful measure.

Terminology

Current is the flow of charges measured in amperes. Electric energy is carried by moving electrons in a wire (measured in coulombs). Charges move only between two points that have PD (potential difference). Work has to be done to move electric charges between two points in unit time (measured in volts).

Electric power measured in wattage refers to a rate of energy generated or spent. A 100 watt bulb is turned on for 1 hour, and then energy utilized is 100 watt-hour. If you know volt and ampere, wattage can be calculated using this formula. The solar panels have markings that specify power output in wattage or voltages. In electricity, circuits require polarity (positive and negative ends) and potential difference for current passage.

How Does Light Become Electricity?

Traveling negatively charged particles, known as electrons, is the key to electricity. These electrons or ions have a small amount of negative charge. The circuitry is installed to facilitate smooth movement of ions. Scientific principles or laws are applied while setting up the wiring. The flow is controlled through an on-off mechanism of switches.

These switches, plug or socket points, and regulators, are made of insulating materials. The copper wiring is usually hidden from the naked eye. The electric/electronic components like charge controller, inverter, battery, etc., are put in protective enclosures. Ventilated plastic boxes or wooden cabinets/shelves are customarily used. Conversion of photons or light energy into electrical energy is not possible without this complicated installation.

Energy Conversion

Energy exists in different forms, and it is closely related to heat and work. According to the law of conservation of energy, it can neither be created nor destroyed; however, energy can be converted from one form to another through the natural or human agency. Plants store radiant energy from the sun in chemical energy (glucose/sugar). This phenomenon is the result of a natural process known as photosynthesis.

Humans apply observation skills and intelligence to understand the natural phenomenon. Science and energy studies have progressed very far in recent centuries. As a result, we convert various forms of energy into one another for our benefit. They include:

- **Automobiles -** Petrol or diesel powers the car. Chemical energy changes into kinetic or mechanical energy (using a battery - electrical energy).

- **Steam Engines -** Conversion of coal or chemical energy into thermal/heat energy. Heat is converted into mechanical energy in turbines to move trains.

- **TV -** Electrical energy is converted into sound and light energy.

In this manner, a large number of energy conversions happen on a daily basis. Human progress and civilization have sped up due to energy utilization; however, rampant energy consumption has affected the global climate. Natural or alternative energy sources like sunlight and wind are considered healthier. Advanced scientific research and engineering precision led to the development of PV panels. Nanotechnology breakthroughs are leading to more and more efficient solar power systems.

How do PV or Solar Cells Work?

The PV panels have solar cells made up of silicon material. Personnel then place positive and negative type of silicon films under a thin sheet of glass. The light from the sun knocks off electrons as the semiconducting nature of the material is very conducive. These free electrons move around the circuits producing the required electric current. The solar power is also stored temporarily in batteries as chemical energy. It is redistributed to the main supply as alternating current (AC) through an inverter.

As batteries store only in the DC form, conversion needs inverters. They convert DC into AC and supply the current through wiring inside the home. Sunlight acts as a trigger to excite and loosen the electrons for free flow or movement. Engineers design these PV panels based on the principles of semiconductor physics. They use computers to design and manufacture the most effective solar panels for home use, but even a local electrician knows how to set up the solar power system on the roof.

Solar Panels

Solar panels incorporate individual solar cells. Semiconductor materials like silicon fabricate these cells. The cells are connected to generate the desired power output or voltage. The batteries are rated in amps (current) in full sunlight. Volts have to be multiplied by amps to find out the watts.

The DC generated in the 12 volts range is stored in a battery. An inverter can directly convert it into AC. In this arrangement, the homeowner can plug into a 120 volts socket for power usage. Alternatively, the battery size has to be chosen by the energy demands of a house. Customers usually opt for the right battery, charge controller and inverter for best performance.

Solar cells are very fragile; therefore, one should handle them with care. The solar company delivers panels with frames and glass covering. Some fixtures also have plexiglass coverings to lower the costs. Glass is more efficient mainly if the sunlight is warm and welcoming. Cells are connected in a panel in -ve,

+ve series with polarized terminals. A standard solar panel layout relies on 3-inch X 6-inch solar cells.

The assembled panels are enclosed in frames and covered in glass. These parts are shifted to the roof and installed with the necessary wiring. The panels are arranged in a continuous array without any gaps whatsoever. The wires also connect the battery, controller, and inverter. After completing the set-up, the electrician usually tests the installation. He uses a digital meter or voltmeter to check output power.

The panels have to capture a right amount of high-quality sunlight directly so they are positioned angularly to receive the light. If panels are not angled correctly, the rays are not received well; therefore, reduces the efficiency, and the voltmeter shows low voltage. The best panels in direct sunlight can assure up to 18 volts of power output any day.

Panels and battery connect to the charge controller at the terminal points. The wiring is insulated to protect against overload or short circuit; hence, this ensures that a fuse will blow in case of an emergency or unexpected fluctuations. Otherwise, the wires get overheated and melt or start a fire. Finally, the inverter is also connected to supply AC power inside the house. Once the whole power system is installed fully, the usage of appliances becomes safe.

System Working & Maintenance

- The up and running system taps the sun's light through the solar panels.
- The panels are activated, and electrons run around loosely and freely.
- The circuits come into play, and charges flow through the wiring.
- The direct current flows into the battery unit in a controlled manner.
- It is stored in the form of chemical energy (acid batteries have immersed metal plates).
- The appropriate polarity is maintained throughout the terminal points, which ensures current conversion from DC to AC through the inverter.
- Finally, one can safely use the sockets and switches inside the home.

Chapter 3: How To Know What Is Right For You?

Solar Power And Climate

Modern consumers are very conscious of energy conservation and environmental protection. Solar panels are a green solution as they do not require traditional forms of electricity; however, sunlight is a compulsory requirement in the efficient functioning of PV panels. Some believe that cold countries or those places with sub-zero temperatures are not suitable; however, with advancements in technology this is becoming irrelevant. Some locations do not welcome bright light, and they are ruled out.

Tropical to temperate climate zones are ideal for setting up solar power systems. Peak sunlight hours are an essential criterion; however, lower amounts of sunlight are not a deterrent either. Consumers can opt for a large number of panels on the roof to compensate for limited sun exposure. The vital calculation pertains to wattage spent per hour or on a daily, weekly, monthly, or annual basis.

Light And Heat

Solar energy from the sun is made up of both light and heat energies. Solar cells technology depends on light or photons. More sunlight or very high temperatures does not assure efficiency of power generation. Since heat accompanies the light, the protection and functionality of various parts are significant. Excess heat can create resistance in the solar power system so the right balance has to be deduced between the two for a higher power output.

Choose the best type of solar cells from the following two main categories:

- **Crystalline Silicon Solar Cells (Monocrystalline or Polythene crystalline)** - They are more efficient and durable, but require mounted panels. More suited for high-temperature regions.

- **Thin Film Solar Cells -** They are less efficient due to the lower amount of silicon material; however, they are inexpensive and allow flexible installation away from a roof.

Note: Temperature coefficient relates solar cell power output loss to heat. The overall panel performance is more efficient for lower coefficients.

Location And Position

Another important criterion is the living arrangements or housing estate. Those who have an independent home without a large roof overhead are ideal candidates. The number of panels and design of panel fixtures can be optimized for efficient energy generation. Cost estimates, however, have to be taken into consideration beforehand. Those who live in flats and apartments have to look into local regulations and co-operation obviously.

Technical Criteria

You can come up with a decision of whether you are a suitable candidate for a solar power system using these guidelines:

1. ***Energy Needs***

- Look at your home's energy needs from the previous utility bills.
- (Hourly energy needs * peak sunlight hours)/panel wattage = the number of panels.
- Make use of low (150W) and high wattages (370W) to fix a suitable range.
- Consult a solar power expert if you are not sure of returns on investment.

2. *Cost Efficiency*

- Householders require between 200 to 2000 kilowatt-hours per month of energy.
- Cost estimates have to factor in installation, maintenance, and repairs.
- Connect the PV system to the local grid with the help of a power company.
- As the weather is unpredictable, you should also consider regular power bills.
- Expensive solar power systems are more efficient and weatherproof.

- An average householder has to spend about $15,000 on installation.
- Federal tax laws can permit homeowners a to obtain green tax credits
- Remember, batteries and inverters have a warranty of 25 and 30 years respectively.

3. Size

- Have clarity of your energy needs - qualitatively and quantitatively.
- Inspect and confirm the suitability of roof shape, size, and angle for installation.
- Larger panels (6 feet) are the best choice for big roofs without any shade.
- PV cells have standard dimensions of around 6 inches X 6 inches.
- Average householders may have to opt for 5.5 feet X 3.25 feet models.

4. Ratings

- Standard panels are thoroughly tested, rated, and labeled or marked.

- Check both standard and PV application test conditions, i.e., STC and PTC.
- These ratings are expressed in wattage in the range of 70 to 300 watts.
- A difference of 50W between STC and PTC takes away almost 3/4th efficiency.
- Efficiency is rated by power output per area, while the price per watt is also vital.

Selection of Suitable Solar Power System

Inexperienced homeowners fail to decide for or against solar power. They do not fully understand the technical aspects or applications. Also, they also worry about costs and maintenance needs. Select the ideal PV system for your home using these instructions:

Your Energy Needs - Calculate your energy needs without fail. You have to know the wattage per hour of spending in the house. Select the suitable panels that are marked with power output values. Match the wattage to the total number of panels and their correct sizes. For example, laptops need at least 25W to deliver a trickle charge.

Panels And Space - If a 120W panel is enormous for your area, choose two 60W panels. The width, thickness, length, material, and power ratings are all necessary.

Big or Small Budget - Efficient panels are costly, while rigid panels are cheaper (per W) as compared to flexible, folding models. Negotiate a deal with the company, and compute the total cost including cables, junction boxes, packaging, manual, etc.

Any Accessories - Mounting racks, brackets or frames are necessary parts. Pole and angled mounts are expensive. Some PV systems are offered with in-built cabling and plug and play connectors.

Type Of Installation – Low-weight folding panels are flexible and transportable. These are more suited for traveling lifestyles. The non-portable, fixed installations are for housing property, sheds and garages.

Quick Calculations

- In 4 hours of temperate sunshine, a 10W panel can assure up to 40W of power.
- However, the same 10W panel can yield about 10W of solar power in the winter season.
- The daytime sunshine has to be up to 6 hours for efficient power generation.
- Household appliances have wattage labels, and you know the number of hours of use.
- Add up the daily watt-hour requirements for the TV, fan, bulb, etc., to get a total.
- Calculate for one season (summer) the total energy needs also in wattage.
- Also find a right battery, panel size and charge controller for your energy needs.

Matching Needs And Solutions

Homeowners do not have identical or similar energy needs. Different people have different lifestyles and habits. The number of family members are different, and outsiders cannot predict power consumption. Yes, electricity bills from the company are useful in knowing the energy needs; however, some residents are responsible, and they save energy through responsible behavior.

Others are not particular about energy conservation, and they are quite wasteful. Solar power has been unveiled in the marketplace for this reason. The natural energy source or sun has abundant light for everyone's needs, but consumers have to make good use of this valuable solution. They have to match their energy needs with solar panel design or layout.

Case Study

Consider a typical American family with a couple and

two children. They live in a moderate house with three bedrooms. This average household spends about 12 to 18 kWh of energy on a daily basis. Luckily, they receive a healthy dose of direct sunlight on the roof of their home. A power system of 1kW would be enough to generate 4 to 5kWh of energy per day.

The government encourages citizens who depend on renewable energy sources. Since sunlight and solar power are green, the family receives a rebate. They have a grid-connected system, and the tariff rates deliver an excellent credit. The homeowner not only saves on energy bills, but also contributes to excess energy. The power company also allows usage of the stored energy for home use so this ideal family has multiple power sources, namely:

- Regular grid-supplied power from the company with a metered monthly bill.
- Solar power from a PV panel system, battery, and inverter for daily use.
- Excess energy diverted to the power company through a grid-connected installation.

The homeowner has the opportunity to lower his monthly bill. He also has the chance to adjust his credit based on excess energy diverted to the grid. The energy capture and spending are metered and tracked for accurate readings. This assures no discrepancy regarding monthly bills, tariff, and regulation policies. The family of four enjoys their stay in the cozy home with uninterrupted power supply.

The children get to enjoy their video games on the latest laptop. This device requires somewhere between 20 to 30 volts for charging needs. The bulbs, fans, coolers, fridge, and ovens receive good quality power without any problems. The family's power requirements are completely satisfied by this arrangement with the power company.

The initial costs of purchases and installation are undoubtedly high; however, this is a wise and valuable investment in the end. There is no need to worry about power outages, and the credit policy assures cost efficiency. Batteries and inverters are expensive, but they have a long life up to 20 years. The system does not require any high maintenance other than cleaning and keeping everything in order.

Chapter 4: Calculating Your Energy Consumption And Sizing Needs

Sizing requirements of solar panels change according to the energy consumption you desire. Here are all the major applications where you need to calculate energy consumption and understand the required size of solar panels.

a. Electronic devices

When finding sizing needs for electronic devices, focus on the following factors:

The energy required by the device

First of all, you need to know the energy required to run your device for a specified period. Most devices provide power usage in watts. You need to multiply this given value by the number of hours you desire to use your device every day. This will inform you about the daily energy required to use your electric device.

Energy generated by a particular solar panel

The next thing to calculate is the energy generation capacity of a solar panel. Here, you will also have to see the power in watts. This is the energy that your device will receive via solar panels; however, it comes down to the time of sunlight exposure too so keep that in mind. Now, multiply the power generation capacity of solar panels and match it with batteries you have.

Finally, you can include weather conditions according to the time of year and match it with your energy consumption requirements. This will provide you a precise number related to power, which you can incorporate when selecting a solar panel size.

b. RVs and Campers

Solar energy is the ultimate solution for campers and RVs. They provide necessary energy consumption to ensure power to your lights and other devices; however, there are multiple factors you should always remember when calculating energy consumption and size of solar panels for camping purposes.

The output provided by a solar panel

Become aware of the output that your solar panel can offer for your RV. This will help you know the energy budget, as well as the time associated with energy availability.

Geographic location

You will have to take your geographical location into account too, as campers keep on changing locations. You need to calculate energy availability according to the sunlight availability in locations where you plan to go.

Devices you have in your RV

Air conditioner, lights, and many other devices

require different power. On average, you can obtain a solar kit for your RV that offers 380 watt power to run general devices; however, the size will increase depending on what kind of devices you have in your RV. Similarly, you also have to care about the potential period for which you desire to use your devices in the RV.

Apart from that, make sure you include battery capacity in amp hours to understand consumption. Large loads require a higher storage capacity to run smoothly.

Now, you can take the amp hour of a battery and multiply it with the solar power capacity according to the time of sunlight, and then match it with the energy required to run your RV devices for a particular period every day. When these two numbers match, you will find the perfect size of panels for your needs.

c. Boats

Boats are a little complicated regarding solar energy consumption calculation. You naturally start with power consumption calculation here as well; however, there are unique factors associated with this calculation.

Solar panel size for topped-off batteries

With regards to the energy consumption required when you are not using your boat, some people don't need any energy when a boat is not in use; however, others have pump, lights or alarm systems that require energy. Some boats can also contain refrigerators or other equipment that require excess energy consumption. You have to incorporate all these factors associated with your energy consumption.

If you need energy just for auto-discharge of batteries, then you can go with small panels of 5 watt size for every battery you have. Make sure you choose the right type of batteries that offer necessary storage.

Solar panel size for bilge pump and other minor permanent loads

In case your boat requires permanent energy consumption, you need to upgrade your solar panel size; however, it will depend on the size of your boat too. The vessel size, cockpit and deck size will help you choose an approximate size, such as 10W, 20W or a higher power size.

You can multiply the amp hour of the battery with the sunlight period, and then you can choose a complementing size that offers the necessary energy to your permanent loads. For instance, if a 20W panel receives sunlight for about 5 to 6 hours every week, you can get proper energy for 120Ah batteries.

Solar panel size for equipment that needs high energy

If your boat has a refrigerator or any other energy-expensive equipment, you need to upgrade your solar panel size. Here, you need to care about the energy efficiency of the equipment. Old equipment requires a higher amount of power in your boat and you need to make sure that solar panel size can compensate for the energy required to run those devices in your boat.

Solar panel size when you are away from land

If you use your boat for long hours away from land, you need to ensure you can consume enough energy and have it available. Calculate the energy requirements of your boat's essentials, and then calculate the hours for which you need energy on a daily basis. That is how you will find a clear solar panel size and battery storage requirement for your boat.

d. House

Reducing your carbon footprint, improving energy efficiency and saving money are all possible with solar panel installation in your home; however, it all comes down to how you calculate energy consumption.

You will require peak sunlight hours, household energy necessity on an hourly basis and wattage of each panel. Multiply the hours with energy requirement and divide it with the wattage of one panel. This way, you will find the number of solar panels required in your home. You can choose a low or high wattage panel ranging from 150W to 370W. These are average power wattage that works for households. You will require between 18 to 40 panels to generate about 10,000 to 11,000 kWh every year. All these calculations will depend on the following factors:

Current kWh consumption in your household

Look at the electricity bills you are paying for the last few months. This illustrates a better concept of energy consumption in your home. Divide the value provided in the bill with 30 to get the daily energy requirement. Multiplying this per day consumption with 365 will give you the energy consumption for the whole year. On average, a medium-sized home requires about 200 kWh every month.

A size that suits your home design

Apart from the numbers, the size of the panels matters too. For that, you need to give a close look at your roof location. It is all about achieving the desired output with maximum sunlight exposure. A limited area in your roof will restrict your ability to get larger sizes; however, you can compensate by choosing higher efficiency panels in small sizes.

For residential purposes, you can find approximately 60 inches by 40 inches; however, the sizes differ depending on the manufacturer you choose.

e. Business

For businesses, energy efficiency and availability are essential and the calculation of power consumption and sizes matters the most.

A small or medium business can use up to 25,000 kWh of energy on an annual basis. This much energy consumption requires correctly-sized panels in suitable numbers, but the energy consumption increases with the size of your business and you need to understand the current business size and potential growth in the coming future as well. This way, you can find the potential energy consumption for your business.

On average, you can obtain 250 watts of power from

your solar panel; however, it is essential to get an accurate energy generation value to multiply and find the number of panels you will require. The size of the panel and the location will also impact this calculation so keep that in mind too.

Most calculations depend on the peak sunlight you obtain in your business location. Mostly, this ranges from 4 to 6 hours on an average day so make sure you calculate the peak sunlight availability, and then define your panel size requirement accordingly.

It is essential to understand the real-world scenarios when calculating energy consumption. On paper, you can obtain average calculations, but the real values are achievable when you record real-world situations along with the variables such as clouds, shades, period, reduced performance of batteries and others. Always include a few extra panels in the desired size to compensate for those variables. This way, you can avoid an unnecessary struggle when you need solar energy. Choose quality panels and balance them with the numbers that can comfortably provide your required energy. That is the right and the most efficient way of calculating panel requirement. Make sure you use the right methods of installation.

Chapter 5: How Much Does It Cost and Where Do I Buy It?

You can take an average value of about $15,000 to $30,000 in your mind with solar panels that provide 4 to 8kW. However, there are a variety of factors to care about when calculating solar panel cost. The type of device you have, the size of the panels, the kind of solar panels and many other aspects help you understand an accurate price.

Basic solar system elements

There are four major elements associated with any solar system.

1. Solar panels

Solar panels, as you already know, receive sunlight energy and change it into electrical energy. The prices of solar panels can differ according to the size and quality you choose. The number of panels will also impact the overall price you pay for the panels, plus, your cost will differ depending on the type of solar panel you select for your needs.

2. Batteries

Batteries work as a storage device for the energy converted by the solar panels. These batteries are essential and provide different storage capacities according to their amp charging range. You calculate the charging capacity and decide the number of batteries required for necessary storage. This adds to the cost of an overall solar system in your place.

3. Controller

Batteries can't manage the current flow without a controller. This device is an essential part of the solar system you acquire and regulates the flow of current electricity. This takes a little part of the overall cost you pay for the system; however, it is essential to calculate the price of a controller when you are deciding your budget.

4. Inverter

The energy stored in the batteries is of no use without your inverter. This device completes the cycle by changing the stored energy to the required voltage, and then this converted voltage reaches the load or equipment.

Therefore, you will have to consider all the four elements mentioned at the time of cost calculation. Also, consider the maintenance and replacement requirement as well. Batteries usually come with a limited lifespan and require replacement. Knowing this will help you understand the ROI of your invested money in solar power. Finally, you can add up to $1 installation cost for every 1W. Executing it describes more clarity with an accurate price.

Value of a reliable manufacturer

Choosing a reputable manufacturer is essential to make a cost-effective investment in solar power. You can follow the written steps below for successful manufacturer selection:

Step 1- Make a list of manufacturers

There are local, national and global level companies offering solar panels, and comparison is the only way you can avoid a wrong investment or too much investment in solar panels. Make your list of solar providers, including necessary information such as prices, power, size, and assurance.

Step 2- Inspect the features provided by the manufacturer

Some companies offer a more extensive variety of solar panels than others; plus, some provide maintenance, but others don't. These features are essential to evaluate before making your final decision.

Step 3- Compare company credentials

Company credentials are the next important aspect you need to care about. Evaluate every manufacturer one by one to understand their market reputation. The popularity of their product will assure you about the quality. You can also look at the certifications associated with the solar panel quality and efficiency. Make sure those credentials match to the needs you have in mind.

Step 4- Analyze product reviews online

There is a lot of information available in the digital world and, thanks to the customer reviews you can learn almost everything about a solar panel manufacturer. Read as many reviews as you can until you are satisfied with the information available about every solar panel choice.

Step 5 - Get a quote

If possible, ask for a quote for your solar panel requirement. This way, you will get a clear idea of the overall price that matches your needs. Most companies provide a quote to help you calculate solar panel prices.

Follow every step and you will know which manufacturer is the best suited to buy solar panels.

Different Types of Panels

When looking for solar panels, you will come across multiple categories. These types are the result of years of research and development, and you can pick from different options that today's market offers. However, they all come with specific traits and disadvantages. Decide the usability of a solar panel type by the benefits you seek.

Here are four major types of panels you can find out there:

1. Monocrystalline

This one is the most used and the original type of solar panels. The cells are created by cutting silicon in a cylinder-like shape. Multiple cells are combined to provide a single panel. These types of panels offer approximately 20% efficiency in practical use.

Pros

Highly advanced silicone material makes the construction of these panels reliable. They come with impressive efficiency or performance rate, which can reach up to 20 to 21%.

When you compare monocrystalline ones with others, it wins with exceptional scores. Smaller sizes provide a better and higher power supply, which allows you to save a lot of space.

These panels work fine, even where light is low, and that is why most manufacturers offer around 25 years of warranty on these types.

You can count on the following pros for this panel type:

- Highly reliable efficiency.
- Easily optimizable for commercial purpose.
- Longer lifespan.

Cons

The most significant disadvantage of this panel type is

the price. The higher lifespan and quality makes them expensive.

Along with that, any obstruction to a panel can lead to circuit breakdown in some cases, plus, the performance level depends on the temperature. Warm weather is best suited for this type, but the performance capacity decreases if the temperature starts rising too much.

However, the only problem you need to worry about is:

- Costly

2. Polycrystalline

Polycrystalline panels are also manufactured by using silicon; however, the shape of these panels looks a little different than the monocrystalline ones. The liquid silicon is poured into a pre-designed mold to get a perfect panel shape. These panels provide up to 14 to 16% efficiency; however, this efficiency also depends on the manufacturing quality.

Pros

The temperature rating is not much lower than the monocrystalline ones so you can invest in these panels. Also, they don't require as much investment as the previous ones so homeowners, businesses, and other places can get cost-effective panel solutions.

Overall pros of polycrystalline panels include:

- Budget-friendly

Cons

The efficiency rating is much lower than the monocrystalline ones. You can only get 14 to 16% of efficiency from these types.

Along with that, you will have to provide a huge space at the time of panel installation. The lower efficiency affects the space utilization of the panels.

These panels are also sensitive to really high temperatures. That is why you can't rely on them for a longer lifespan.

All in all, these are the disadvantages of

polycrystalline panels:

- It has high temperature sensitivity.
- It has a much lower rate of efficiency than monocrystalline.
- It takes a larger space for the desired electric energy.
- It works for a smaller period.

3. Thin-film

These types are created by layering multiple films of photovoltaic elements. These elements can be organic cells or amorphous silicon.

Pros

These panels provide a lightweight option for panel seekers. There are no issues associated with obstructions and shading. These types work fine, even where the lights don't reach properly, and you can have them for a long time.

So, the advantages come down to:

- Lower costs
- Easy production
- Flexibility in installation

Cons

Some disadvantages restrict the popularity of thin-film panels. Its efficiency and lifespan are the two major concerns that people have in mind. The efficiency rate never goes higher than 10%. Mostly, you can achieve 7 to 8% of efficiency from such panels. That is what impacts the warranties of these types too.

So, you have to worry about:

- Low-efficiency rate
- Limited warranties
- Unreliable lifespan
- Large space requirement

4. Concentrated PV cell

These types are the ultimate solution for advanced solar power requirements. You can receive about 40 to 41% of efficiency, which is suitable for businesses and commercial purposes.

Pros

The efficiency rate is the most prominent advantage that you can have with these types of panels. The performance level is also admirable, which allows you to rely on these panels for a long time.

You can choose CVPs for the following reasons:

- It has exceptional efficiency.
- It has outstanding performance.
- It has long-term durability.

Cons

Although their disadvantages are negligible in this

case, you have to balance these panels with a cooling system and solar tracker. These are required to achieve the maximum efficiency rate possible with CVP panels. Apart from that, there is nothing to worry about.

So, the disadvantages include:

- Installation of a cooling system.
- Installation of a solar tracker.

It is important to remember that every type is suitable for one or the other purpose, so you should judge their pros and cons according to your requirements.

Chapter 6: How Do I Know Where To Put My Panels?

The location of the solar panel is a critical factor to get the maximum efficiency after installation. It becomes vital that you don't pick a random place of installation. Focus on all the following factors when choosing a location for solar panel installation.

a. The roof's condition

Mostly, people think about installing their panels on the roof; however, the state of your roof should be in top-notch condition. A solar panel can provide years of durability but, if your roof is not able to match their performance, you might have to invest in re-installation, which is why most panels get damaged.

To save yourself from such issues, it would be wise if you inspect the roof's condition in advance. Make sure that the materials and layout of the roof are capable of maintaining the panels for a long time. If not, make the possible changes first.

b. Direction

The exposure to sunlight decides the energy generation in the case of solar panels so you need to choose a direction that provides maximum sunlight exposure. Inspect the obstacles in every direction. Tall buildings, mountains, and trees usually restrict the sunlight exposure. Make sure you choose a direction free from such barriers.

c. Angle

The location of your place decides the peak sunlight availability. For instance, the south areas get the maximum sunlight, which increases the chances of energy production and, as your location moves towards the north, the energy creation capacity decreases so you need to know your geographical location and match it with the orientation of your place. Find out what latitude tilt you have, and then use this information to decide a suitable angle for your panels.

To find an angle for a 25 degrees latitude, you need to tilt the panels with the same angle in the direction of the sun. So, for 25 degrees latitude, you will need a tilt of 25 degrees in the latitude, and then you have to increase 5 degrees for every 5 degree increase in the latitude. This is only applicable until you reach 40 degree latitude. After that, your latitude number will get an additional 20 degrees. So, for 55 degrees latitude, you will have to place the panel at a 75 degree tilt angle.

The angle selection can seem difficult for many people, and it is advised that you hand over the job to professionals who know your location and understand sunlight exposure.

d. Distance between panels

The next thing you need to care about is the distance. Every panel needs to stay at a certain distance. Usually, this distance tends to be about four feet;

however, you need to consult a professional to understand the distance required for your place and purpose.

e. Temperature

The heat reduces the efficiency of a solar panel, and that is why you need to make sure that solar panels don't get too warm. The electrons get slower if the heat goes out of control. This reduces the capacity of solar cells to convert energy. Mostly, the heat maintenance depends on the quality you choose, but you need to make sure that the location of installation doesn't increase the temperature of the panels too much. Choose a reliable panel if you desire to get the maximum energy generation during afternoons.

f. Shading

You know that shades are not suitable for solar panels at all. Higher shading leads to lower energy generation, but the problem here is that shades in a location can change on a daily and seasonal basis. That is why you have to be careful when deciding the installation location for panels.

You already have the idea about barriers in your area. Now, you have to think about the height, size, and distance of those barriers. The idea is to choose the most efficient place and direction for the panels where shading doesn't harm the quality of the energy generation. Try to obtain maximum exposure at the time of peak sunlight hours. This is when your panels will create maximum energy. Take into account all those components that you have on your roof. Their shades can also impact the energy generation.

Get rid of the unnecessary objects on your roof. Trim those trees that become a problem for light exposure. A few trees never impact the sunlight. It only happens when you have many trees in one place.

Try to reduce the shading as much as possible to provide maximum sunlight to the panels. If the angle is correct, they will produce the desired amount of energy for sure.

g. Dirt and dust

Dirt and dust accumulation reduces the sunlight exposure. Apparently, it leads to reduced energy creation via solar panels. A location where debris keeps on accumulating is not suitable for your panels. The sunlight won't reach the cells, which will never let you have the amount of energy you have been looking for.

If your area doesn't get proper rain for a long time, this can cause dry weather conditions. Dry weather increases the issue of dirt and dust. Also, if your place is near to a construction area, your solar panel will have difficulties creating power. The options would be to avoid such locations. If this is not possible, make sure your panels get regular maintenance to keep them operating in peak conditions. You can also contract solar panel cleaners who come with appropriate devices to clean your panels.

Dirt and dust are probably the biggest problems for solar panel owners. They keep on troubling and never let panels provide their maximum performance. Locations with proper rain don't get too much dust in the environment so, if you live in an area where rain manages the environment, you don't have to worry about dirt and dust too much. Of course, maintenance is still required, but not too frequently as it would be in dry weather places. You can call professional maintenance service providers every once in a while and get the work done.

h. Irradiance

You already know that weather conditions keep on changing by the hour. Earth attains different positions with respect to the sun every year, but this is not the only cause of radiation change in the sunlight.

When talking about irradiance, you can say that is the total solar radiation that falls on a described surface so, if the irradiance is high on your solar panel, it improves the energy creation capacity. The issue is that irradiance keeps on changing throughout a particular day. Multiple factors, such as the sun's earth's position, haziness in the weather, clouds and even air pollutants, impact the irradiance.

On an annual basis, you can expect a variation of 5 to 10% of the irradiance in a single year, but this is just an average value, as multiple variables act for a particular geographical location.

The point is that you need to think about output projection before choosing a location for installation. Understanding your area for today, tomorrow and the whole year is what informs you about the output projection of solar panels.

A professional team can help with that too. Such teams can measure all the irradiance factors in your area and help you pick the right solar panel and a suitable installation location. Also, professionals will also inform you about the overall energy creation you can expect from your solar panel on an annual basis.

i. Snow

In an area where snow falls, energy creation via solar panel gets affected too. Snow immediately forms a layer on the surface of solar panels and stops panels from getting radiation. If you do not think about this issue in the beginning, you may end up plowing snow three times a day. Alternatively, you will have to leave it to melt on its own.

The installation location should be within your reach. This way, you can quickly remove the layers of snow from your panels; otherwise, it will reduce the estimated energy creation.

Power generation via solar panels is not just a quick installation process. You cannot just focus on today's energy requirement. A wide range of location-related factors work together to give the panels appropriate radiation. All you need to do is understand those factors and decide the location and angle of installation. With that, include your maintenance requirement in the decision-making process too.

It sure seems complicated in the beginning; however, once you follow a systematic installation path, it makes your future energy secured for good. It does not matter if you have a business or want panels in your home. The perfect installation is something that is important for every solar panel owner. If you have many, then the job gets more critical and necessary.

So, make sure you go through all the points mentioned above once more to get a better idea. Incorporate these aspects when you are planning to place your panel. It will help you gain a reliable source of energy throughout the year, and that is precisely what you want, right?!

Chapter 7: How To Set Up Superior Solar Power Systems For Energy Efficiency

1. Introduction

Water, sun, wind, non-renewables, and thermonuclear energy are the various sources of power. Modern societies are dependent upon the grid for their daily electricity. Natural energy is also being used by those who install efficient solar power systems. The contemporary solar panels can provide energy for shops, homes, workshops and swimming pools. The off-grid supply is not always sufficient, and so hybrid solutions are also implemented.

Solar Power System

- The sun at the center of our solar system is the most reliable energy source. It releases immense quantities of heat and light (photons) towards the earth.

- This solar energy is captured using photovoltaic cells and converted into electricity. Panels or arrays are installed carefully to create an electrical circuit.
- Silicon like semiconductor material is used in creating solar cells. They have positive and negative layers and act as a battery.
- Inverters are also installed for DC to AC conversion and ground fault protection. They also track maximum power points and calculate system statistics (metering).
- The solar power system can be typically tied to the local grid. Excess energy is fed back to the grid for cost-effective, future usage.

2. DIY Project

Whether you hire a professional or plan a DIY project, safety is paramount. Doing things by yourself is empowering and liberating in many ways, but electrical works have some valid risks and potential hazards. Follow the best practices and become an informed installer.

Basics

Solar panels generate about 18 volts of power in full sunlight. They use solar charge controllers and photovoltaic (PV) cells. Power inverters are used to convert the stored DC into AC for household appliances. Make sure you are comfortable with volts, wattage, ampere per hour, peak rating, battery reserve capacity, etc. The best PV system estimates can be made using online calculators or software tools (PVsyst, PVWatts v4 NREL, Energy Periscope, Clean Power Estimate, etc.)

Design

These safety considerations are taken into account before starting the PV system set up:

- The design has to satisfy local and state building safety requirements.
- Thorough inspections should yield accurate measurements on the site.
- They include roof dimensions, slope, existing electrical lines and shade analysis.
- Obstacles and safety codes have to be factored into the final design.
- The plan should accommodate a customer's aesthetic taste and power needs.
- The set-up position or location, component and material types are also vital.

Components

- **Solar PV Models -** ISO compliant modules and panels from a trustworthy manufacturer. PV options are flat-plate, terrestrial (thin film or silicon crystalline).
- **Inverters** - Standalone, smart or utility-

interactive systems that comply with IEEE and National Electric Code standards.

- **Mounting Devices/Racking Systems** - Safe products with grounding or bonding paths and mechanical strength. The material should be fire and wind resistant and satisfy building codes.
- **Monitoring System** - A compatible system with 99.5% connectivity, regular performance checking and power availability alerts.
- **Electrical Parts** - Connectors, cables, junction boxes, IP-rated enclosures, and wire positioning devices.

Best Practices

- Procure all the permits and approvals for PV system installation and inspection.
- Ground fault protection should include appropriate electrodes and conductors.
- The solar power system should also have

lighting protection and ground fault detection.

- Components and electrical equipment should be marked or labeled.
- Identifying manufacturer size, type, rating and hazard warnings is crucial.
- The mechanical installation has to factor in wind, snow and load-bearing capacity.
- Aluminum mounting systems are dependable for withstanding wear and tear.
- PV modules should be transported, stored, mounted and connected correctly.
- After system set-up installation, the interconnections have to be approved for use.
- The set-up has to be well documented and ready for operation or maintenance.

Step-By-Step Installation: Off-Grid PV System

Installing a grid-connected system has many challenges and obstacles. The off-grid systems are not a piece of cake either. The installer has to climb a high roof, manage safety issues, and buy expensive components.

Step 1: Load Calculation

The calculations are based on some appliances (fans, TV, and lights) and their running time. An 11 watt CFL bulb for 5 hours requires 55 watt-hour. Add up all the watt-hours to find the total power requirement.

Step 2: Battery Selection

Sunlight is not guaranteed, so the battery is needed for energy storage. Deep cycle, lead-acid batteries with deep slow and partial discharge features are the best. Make sure you calculate power, watt hour, voltage and capacity. The choice is usually between 12, 24, and 48 volts.

Step 3: Best Solar Panels

Expensive monocrystalline panels are more efficient than polycrystalline modules. The 125 watt, 12 volt panels assure 480 watt-hour of total power output (4 hours of sunlight).

Step 4: Superior Charge Controller

They regulate voltage and current between PV solar panel and battery. Excess voltage is converted to amps and charge voltage is optimized for battery storage.

Step 5: Choice Of Inverter

A pure sine-wave inverter converts battery DC to AC for home use. Make sure the power rating is equal to more than the total load in watts at any time.

Step 6: Mounting

Chose the ideal roof location or a stand for mounting

the panels. The sunlight should be bright and without any obstruction in this spot.

Step 7: Connecting

Set up the serial and parallel connections between the various components. Those who are not confident should take an electrician's help.

Step 8: Enclosures

The installer places the inverter and battery in ventilated stands or protective enclosures.

Step 9: Wiring

- DC breaker and meter connect the solar panel to charge controller.
- From here, the output lines go to battery and DC load.
- The battery line runs to the inverter through the meter followed by the DC breaker.

- The installer needs to connect the inverter and the AC load to the AC breaker.

3. Tips to Hire Professionals

Not everyone is comfortable with the panel set-up, electrical circuits and inverters. They may not have the physical capacity or technical understanding to carry out the task. Also, they have to deal with local power suppliers, rules and regulations. Skillful use of tools, risk analysis, optimal positioning, and hazard recognition are very technical. Such challenges quickly prompt some customers from dropping the idea of a DIY project.

They have no other alternative but to hire a competent and professional company.

Challenges

- Householders may not be able to connect the solar power system to the local grid. Building codes and power utility company regulations have to be understood first.

- A sizeable set-up can be expensive, and the customers have to be prepared. Insurance coverage can be helpful, but one should contact the insurers for the confirmation.
- Getting permits from companies and local authorities is not an easy task. Some do not co-operate, while others have a preference for power contractors.
- Purchasing sub-standard components for the installation is counterproductive. The power system may not have well-written manuals or set-up instructions.
- Self-installation also requires the purchase of sophisticated tools. The equipment does not come cheap, and poorly designed installations are not reliable.
- A minimum knowledge of electricity is necessary for setting up solar arrays. DIY projects do not come with a fixed-term warranty either.

Hiring A Company

The customer can hire a trained professional and purchase the solar kit. The better alternative is to approach a reliable, local contractor. There are many benefits of hiring a professional company that specializes in solar power installations.

- Contractors have direct links with traders and wholesalers. They purchase the kits and other equipment in large quantities at lower prices.

- The skilled installers have a rich experience and knowledge of solar panels. They identify the ideal position and bring their tools for installation.

- They are well versed in electrical supply, circuitry, hazards and risks. Safe installations can guarantee the security of the residents and property.

- Minute technical details and safety guidelines are followed to the tee. The installers know all about building, electrical, interconnection, etc., codes and standards.

Tips

- Must do a background check on the contractor's reputation and previous work.
- Modern companies have their websites and 24/7 customer support.
- Professionals are willing to perform an on-site inspection and forward a quote.
- They also honor warranties and deliver a well-designed set-up without any delays.
- The installer not only sets up, but also assures testing and maintenance.
- Solar power system companies have an efficient and broad social network.
- The complete installation unit completes in a phased or planned manner.
- Transparent contractors are upfront about what they can and cannot do.
- Professionals set up a working system and assure repairs or replacements.

4. Conclusion

To summarize, alternative energy sources like solar power systems are efficient, but they have to be safely designed and installed with engineering precision. An individual needs to purchase the most suitable equipment and components. A knowledge of electrical works is essential to avoid risks and potential hazards. Those who can manage load capacity, power requirements and wiring should pursue self-installation.

An off-grid system does not have hassles related to permits and inspections. Standard products, best practices and safety guidelines are mandatory. A Do It Yourself (DIY) project should be carried out in a sequence of steps. The installed PV system has to be tested, inspected, operated and maintained with due care. Those who are not confident have to opt for a professional company. Hire skilled contractors who can install efficient systems.

Chapter 8: Moving Off The Grid

Moving off the grid allows you to depend on solar power energy entirely. Cost-efficiency and a green lifestyle have made this concept highly accessible all over the world.

When thinking about moving off the grid, people ask several questions. The requirements and benefits are majorly associated with such questions. Here are all those questions answered:

a. How much energy do I need?

This question is valid, but the answer can vary depending on your energy needs. A medium-sized home requires about 900kWh energy per month, but you can reduce this energy requirement by smartly installing solar panels.

People don't think about how much energy their appliances are consuming, but calculating these energy requirements is essential when moving off the grid. The first job should be to know the energy required by the water heater, furnace, stove and other appliances.

Make a list of the most energy-consuming appliances

First, create a list that includes all the appliances consuming maximum energy on the grid. These can be:

- Air conditioner
- Lighting
- Refrigerator
- Electric furnace
- Clothes dryer
- Dishwasher
- Oven and others

Thanks to advanced solar panels, you can replace energy source for all of these appliances, but it would be wise to eliminate those that are not so important in your household. This brings us to the next point.

Categorizing loads that are movable "off-grid."

You can get the energy to run the water heater, refrigerator, air conditioner and other appliances, but it widely depends on how much energy you can generate in your area. The real point here is the capacity of solar panels, the available space for installation, and the sunlight exposure throughout the year. This will help you know the total amount of energy you can generate, and then you can decide which electric loads are more important to shift off the grid.

Make a list of smaller electrical appliances

After evaluating your large loads, think about the overall smaller loads in your place. These loads can be small lights, computers, routers and others. Although individually they seem low energy consuming, an overall evaluation is essential.

Move to more energy-efficient appliances

Before moving off the grid, it would be wise to design

your home for solar power. This means that you can choose energy-efficient appliances to re-design your household's energy consumption. Change the lighting, heating system and other components where changes are possible.

You can even think about insulating your place as much as possible to gain maximum energy efficiency.

By considering all the above-mentioned factors, you will reach a better idea of how much energy your place needs when moving off the grid.

b. Can my excess energy flow BACK to the grid if I want?

It depends on the location and utility provider you have. There are areas where net metering is available. This approach allows your excess energy to flow back to the grid (if your solar system is connected to one), and you will obtain credit for that energy.

However, there are states where net metering is not applied, meaning you can't choose to send back the excess energy to the grid, so it would be wise to check whether your state comes under net metering or not.

c. What is the BENEFIT of doing this? How much can the average household save?

Living "off grid" comes with a variety of benefits. It is all about producing power for your needs and using it to the extent you desire.

Reduced monthly energy cost

Saving energy cost is probably the most significant advantage you attain with off-grid power consumption. It is true that you have to make a few initial investments, but the installation is your one-time investment that saves you from future monthly bills.

The savings will depend on your area, home size, energy requirements, etc; however, people can save up to $100 every month by installing solar panels. Most quality panels work fine for more than 20 years so you can get an estimated saving of about $20,000 in most of the major locations.

Apart from that, you can leverage net metering if that is available in your state. You can provide your excess energy to the utility grid and save more money every month, but it will require you to stay connected with a utility grid. Many people find net metering a better idea than living entirely off the grid. This way, energy efficiency becomes possible for the whole location, and you get to save more money every month.

Usually net metering allowing you to “sell” your excess energy that you create back to the grid in the form of an energy credit. Then when you need the energy from the grid (low sunlight, excess energy demands) you don’t actually have to pay for this. There are significant advantages of not going fully off the grid and using net metering.

Safety from blackouts

In many areas, blackouts are a common problem. If you live in such a place, the off-grid power source can save you. Your lights stay bright which ensures the security and safety of your place. Lights will obtain energy from the solar power system; hence, they will operate constantly, as you desire.

Even if blackouts are not an issue, you can feel stress-free about the power availability. Grid power will not matter.

Flexible lifestyle

People who love to stay close to nature love moving off the grid. Gaining freedom from grid power allows you to go about anywhere. You can choose an open space, rural area or a natural surrounding as your home. Solar panels give you your energy to use.

Positive impact on the environment

Many people do care about climate change and global warming. For them, off-grid living is a great way to give back to the earth the protection it deserves. Solar power is renewable, which makes it green. More and more people can reduce the rate of global warming by moving to the grid-free power supply.

Even a single person creates a significant difference regarding environment protection. Using solar power for more than 30 years, you can remove a significant amount of greenhouse gases that contribute to climate change and overall global warming.

Harnessing energy

Solar power is one of the renewable sources of energy that allows you to harness. No matter where you live, you can obtain energy via solar power. You require the appropriate equipment and a connected system; the rest happens automatically.

Harnessing capacity is a benefit that you don't get via other energy sources. The chances of losing energy or receiving less than what you require are higher in other resources. On the other hand, you can design your solar system according to your energy requirements and leverage energy production throughout the year.

Ability to use for diverse purposes

The diversity of energy makes solar power more beneficial for anyone. Solar power generated by the solar panels is changeable into electricity or heat. All you need is a correct system. This enables you to run all kinds of appliances in your home or a commercial place without struggling for power. Solar power is the ultimate source of energy, which works great when you collect enough of it.

Low maintenance required

Solar systems are known for their low maintenance requirement. You need simple cleaning once or twice every year. Of course, it depends on the installation quality you acquire in the first place. Also, you can get affordable cleaning service for the solar panels. Trusted manufacturers offer warranties for their panels, which also allows you to save paying for maintenance costs for a long time. No matter what happens to your solar panels, your manufacturer pays for those damages.

The efficiency of the panels depends on their maintenance. This maintenance also includes the cable quality, as they transfer energy from one part to the other, so you should focus on getting your cables repaired from time to time. Doing this won't cost too much, as compared to what you save in the process of going off-grid.

Consistent development

Solar power is the future of energy consumption as all the big corporations are investing in gaining better technologies in this direction. This means that when you choose to move to solar energy, it enables you to get the latest technology for power generation. Having the latest technology means that you have the best chances of utilizing power and energy.

As the technology grows further, you can upgrade your power system and attain more effectiveness and efficiency. This opportunity is not available with traditional grid energy.

Moving from grid to solar power has unique benefits, and now you know all about them. Understanding these benefits will help you make your final decision. Focus immensely on the quality of lifestyle and cost-saving opportunities. You can have your energy supply and save throughout the year.

Now that you know all about solar power and solar panels, get yourself ready. Choose the best-suited panels, quality manufacturers and utility providers, if you desire. Apply what you have learned here in every way possible to make your daily power consumption efficient and cost-effective. You can begin by finding out the exact energy required and the cost you are supposed to pay for that. Once that is done, move to the further steps of finding solar panels and other components and getting them installed.

I hope that this informational piece has been useful for you. In addition, you will attain a perfect quality solar system as planned and desired.

Like the book? The greatest compliment is leaving a review on Amazon. Thanks in advance ☺

EXTRA BONUS!

Thanks for purchasing *DIY RV Solar Power: How To Install Your Own Solar Power System For Your RV, Camper, or Boat.* As a bonus and thanks, we want to provide you with additional information and content on an on-going basis.

Subscribe now and get a free article, **Seven Tips To Save Energy That NOBODY Does!**

Type the below link in to any browser on any device to for install access to unlock these extra secret that no one knows!

www.bit.ly/freesolaroffer

Simply type the above link into any web browser on any device.

By subscribing above, you will get advanced notifications on future books on this, along with various other Home Improvement topics. You might even be able to get them for free. Don't worry, we won't spam you (that often lol). Plus, you can always unsubscribe whenever you want.

Be sure to check out these other great books on Solar Power. You can order these from Amazon.

SOLAR POWER

HOW TO HARNESS THE SUN TO POWER YOUR LIFE – AND GO OFF-GRID WHILE DOING IT

MIKE HOLSWORTH

SOLAR POWER

MAKING THE SMART SWITCH TO SOLAR POWER – AND STAYING WITHIN BUDGET!

MIKE HOLSWORTH

Made in the USA
Lexington, KY
23 May 2019